lost in
language
SOUND

also by ntozake shange

OR HOW I FOUND
MY WAY TO THE
ARTS: ESSAYS

lost in
language
SOUND

&

Ntozake Shange

ST. MARTIN'S GRIFFIN ✤ NEW YORK

www.stmartins.com

I want to thank those publications where some of these essays first appeared: *Konch,* the *Yardbird Reader, Real News, Black Renaissance Noire, Dance Magazine, The Village Voice,* and *Mr. Wrong: Real-Life Stories About the Men We Used to Love.*

Grateful acknowledgment is made for permission to reprint from the following:

Lyrics from "Can't Touch This." Copyright © 1990 Bust It Publishing/BMI, a div. of EverGreen. Copyrights Jobete Music Co., Inc./ASCAP/Stone Diamond Music Corporation/BMI/Stone City Music/ASCAP. All rights reserved. Used by permission.

Elizabeth Alexander, excerpts from "The Venus Hottentot" from *The Venus Hottentot.* Copyright © 1990 by the Rector and visitors of the University of Virginia. Reprinted with the permission of the author and Graywolf Press, Minneapolis, Minnesota, www.graywolfpress.org.

Lyrics from "Suicide Notes." Copyright © 1968. Reprinted by permission of SLL/Sterling Lord Literistic, Inc. Copyright by Amiri Baraka.

Excerpts from "Words" and "Beautiful Black Women." Copyright © 1969. Reprinted by permission of SLL/Sterling Lord Literistic, Inc. Copyright by Amiri Baraka.

Excerpt from the book *New and Collected Poems.* Copyright © 1988 by Ishmael Reed. Permission granted by Lowenstein Associates, Inc.

Excerpt from *After Colonialism,* edited by Gyan Prakash. Copyright © 1995 by Princeton University Press. Reprinted by permission of Princeton University Press.

Excerpt from "We're Off to See the Wizard" (from *The Wizard of Oz*). Music by Harold Arlen, lyric by E. Y. Harburg © 1938 (Renewed) EMI Feist Catalog Inc. Rights throughout the world controlled by EMI Feist Catalog Inc. (Publishing) and Alfred Music Publishing Co. Inc. (print). All rights reserved. Used by permission of Alfred Music Publishing Co. Inc.

Library of Congress Cataloging-in-Publication Data

Shange, Ntozake.
   Lost in language & sound : or how i found my way to the arts: essays / Ntozake Shange.—1st ed.
      p. cm.
   ISBN 978-0-312-20616-1
   1. Shange, Ntozake.   2. Creation (Literary, artistic, etc.)   3. Creative ability.
I. Title.
   PS3569.H3324Z46 2011
   812'.54—dc23
   [B]

                                                          2011026770

First Edition: December 2011

10   9   8   7   6   5   4   3   2   1

for my beloved friend
Claude Sloan, Jr.
who cares for me.

contents

acknowledgments

i must thank my ever-nurturing editor of some thirty-five years, Michael Denneny, who kept this project alive thru strokes, major surgery & simple chaos. he was able to remember essays i had written but felt a total stranger to, & for that i must thank him. his patience and humor as well as his not insignificant editing have once again brought back whole pieces & fragments foreign to my memory.

in addition i want to thank everyone at Russell & Volkening, my agent for over thirty-five years, who would never let me give up even when i was unable to read or write anything. Tim Seldes, Rosanna Bruno, Jesseca Salky, and Carrie Hannigan have been there for me through every aspect of my illness & continuing recovery.

again Cora Ledet tended to the manuscript as carefully as the Dead Sea Scrolls & i thank her for her meticulous work.

i am also grateful to Quincy Troupe, editor of *Black Renaissance Noire,* for refusing to believe i couldn't find any poems in my stash of papers even though i told him again & again that i couldn't write anything. he said, "well, send me something old." that i could do. the same kind of support came from Ishmael Reed, editor of *Konch,* who specifically wanted old, unpublished poems of mine that he had heard me read before i was ill. & i cannot possibly leave out Maya Angelou, who sent me children's books to read so I would regain that ability, Maya thank you.

everyone at New Dharma Meditation Center for Urban Peace who prayed for me i thank.

finally, i have to thank my family: mami, Eloise O. Williams, Paul T. Williams Jr., my brother, and my sisters, Ifa Bayeza and Bisa Williams. & there's still one more, my beloved daughter, Savannah Shange, whose faith and serenity are hopefully reflected in the following pages.

preface

i've no doubt that inhabiting my mother's womb for all nine months left me twirling & crooning through the placenta & the water I'd yet to break. my father & mother were quite light on their feet & taken with jazz, rhythm & blues, bebop, & the high life. anywhere the colored people were celebrating, my parents celebrated too. & i got to go cause i was still in my mother. so it's no surprise to me that i needed Sun Ra, Cecil Taylor, Prince, Ruth Brown, Duke Ellington, Jeanne Lee & Albertina Walker in order to live. one other special element of language which mother gifted me with was poetry. she could recite & did Sterling Brown, Robert Hayden, Langston Hughes, Paul Laurence Dunbar & many more by heart. i was a blessed child.

i did indeed read books way into the night & neglect friendships for reading at the foot of a grand oak tree. yet i found time to sneak downstairs to watch my parents & friends dance & copy them on the landing. mommy pointed out dancers, like the Nicholas Brothers, Bojangles & Katherine Dunham, whenever she got the chance. i wanted to be that, i wanted to hear that. i imagined the Harlem Renaissance poets were surrounded by music, friends of musicians and had music in their language. it's unavoidable. but it was a different time. the beatniks droned on to clipped bass fiddles, but i saw Jack Kerouac on the Jack Paar show and said to myself, "i could do that." then years later, i heard Archie Shepp reading his own work to his own music & LeRoi Jones reading with the New York Art Quartet, and i said, "i can do that." & that's what my life has been about, language & music & dance. the poetry & music lift me off my feet. i'm not saying i did this on my own. as you read these essays you'll discover how many people helped me shape my vision.

neither am i saying that the black arts movement had no substantial effect on me. i must confess to a certain hero worship of Toomer, Baraka & Reed. what i learned from them is immeasurable & still manifest even in my current work & i am not conscious of it. then there's dear Pedro Pietri, my longtime friend, who has made the transition to another plane. Pedro helped me find a cutting humor & political edge in my work which i hadn't caught before. then there was the late Ted Joans who made the language jazz itself & devilish at once. these are the places i lived, never forgettin Jackie Wilson sliding cross the stage on his knees or Tina Turner shake that thang, or Bo Diddley with his nasty guitar, & so many more.

when we lived in Trenton, which was sposed to be an industrial town, it was really country. Big Ed's Eggerts Crossing Inn even hosted Brook Benton & the late James Brown. there we could dance, gorge ourselves on ribs, fried chickens, bunches of collard greens, a side of beef, or peach pie. once we got to St. Louis everything changed. i didn't have to play around with the radio to get a signal from a colored station in Newark. there were several colored radio stations in St. Louis itself. i could walk to the library & find books by negro authors with no trouble at all. the pharmacist was colored, the grocery store on the corner was colored. my neighbors were colored & my age. so we danced & sang songs that worked their way up from Memphis & down from Detroit. we heard everything & everybody. Baby Washington, Sonny Til, the Clovers, the Ink Spots, everybody. all the while going to integrated schools, colored as we wanted to be.

meanwhile, my father was still immersing himself & me in Fletcher Henderson, the Kansas City Six, & Xavier Cugat. later came Milt Jackson, Oscar Peterson & Mary Lou Williams. nobody on the scene escaped us. daddy wasn't being paid with fresh produce anymore. he was a resident at the black hospital, Homer G. Phillips, where my mother worked as a social work administrator. we were nonetheless having our horizons continually pushed. when my parents traveled, which they did a lot, they brought the music & dance back with them. i remember my father practicing surgical knots from the side of a congo drum from Cuba. i remember Beny More & Machito, La Lupe, & the late Celia Cruz & the late Tito Puente. i heard them way into the night when daddy worked on his medical charts & in the morning when he was involved with his toilette & we were eating our breakfasts. then i began to stretch out to the sounds my father was not quite ready for. he seemed to be unable to hear past Clifford Jordan & Art Blakey, while i was immersed in Coltrane, Tyler & Shepp, Colón, Ismael Quintana, La India, & Tito Allen. i did get him to an Art Ensemble of Chicago concert, a Cecil Taylor unit performance, but that was as far as it went. he liked Air (the late Fred Hopkins & Steve McCall & the very present Henry Threadgill), as well as David Murray & Arthur Blythe.

my mother supported my every venture in dance, attending classes with Titos Sompa, Loremil Machado & the great Dianne McIntyre. mommy didn't even say much about me taking class till my seventh month of pregnancy when i pulled a muscle & took that as a sign to slow down.

to this day i am still experimenting with language & sound. a matter of fact, a few years ago i had a reading in Washington, D.C. & was on my way in when i saw Joe Bowie of Defunkt. i asked him if he would do this job with me, he said yes. next thing i knew we were onstage after having reviewed two poems. but our history together included extemporaneous conversation. so Joe & I cracked jokes before the poems, at the middle of the poems & at the end of the poems. the show went over marvelously. working with Kahil El'Zabar & the Ethnic Heritage Ensamble has led to even more of a freeness inside the music itself. & the work I do with my former husband, David Murray, astounds me. sometimes I say to him, "we shouldn't have gotten married, we should have had a band." this is what I wanted you to know before you read these essays. it's not that I'm a recluse, it's that my intimates are words & notes.

i.

from analphabetic
to script obsessed

LIKE MOST PEOPLE OF COLOR, BLACK PEOPLE IN THE New World, I came by my passion for literature in a circuitous way, a night journey marked by music, movement, improvisation, and smells of perfume, sweat, and humid star-flickering nights. I pay tribute and homage, first to the wonderous miracle of language on an African's tongue. My house, my neighborhood, my soul was immersed as far as I can recall in the accents of Togo, Liberia, Trinidad, Costa Rica, Chicago, Lagos, New Orleans, Bombay, and Cape Town, not to minimize in any way drawls of the Mississippi, clipped consonants from Arkansas, or soprano-like chisme (gossip) of Kansas City. So, first, the voices of my people made me want to have the sounds forever. To rid my world of silence, the prohibited, the stiff, and the mendacious.

A kitchen, a back porch somewhere, or the back of the bus opened rhythmic and lyrical realms to me in the same way that the shuffle of shoes brought music to Miles Davis' ear. Maybe it's the land we, me & Miles, were raised on, or the river, or what Henry Dumas called the "Ark of Bones" floating in the deep dank Mississippi that lent our spirits to the whispers of our landscapes. I'm not always sure, but I am convinced the constant flow of black folks from all over through St. Louis left an indelible impression on me: my sense of rhythm, melody, irony, and beauty come from that earth, that river.

But, no, that's not all the truth. Some of my sense of language fell from my mother's lips at dusk or Sunday morning, when thanks to her elocution classes, Miss Ellie recited Dunbar, Cullen, Hughes, Sterling, Brown, and Alice Walker as naturally as breaking into song which she also did, sometimes. Remembering that these words from those poets sauntered though the air, remember too that Tito Puente, La Lupe, Jackie Wilson, the Shirelles, Dizzy Gillespie, and Charlie Parker entered my world just as freely, only it was when my father, Dr. P. T., came home that bebop, rhumbas and rhythm & blues became the vernacular of the house, the common dialect of relations with the world and myself.

With music came movement because we were colored and southern. Dance was something we did like other folks walk, or sip coffee, I imagine.

Later on I sought out language that somehow echoed inarticulate, inchoate impulses I lived with, in the same way I watched Camen de Lavallade's body make sense of an irrational vicious place I was supposed to pledge allegiance to every day. Between, James Baldwin with *The Fire Next Time* and *The Amen Corner,* I confused Pearl Primus, Katherine Dunham, and Eartha Kitt defying the limitation of the body and the English language with an art that was rightfully mine, an art I could claim, from which I could spring like Jesse Owens at the starting line.

As a young adult, I discovered beatniks and some black ones like LeRoi Jones (Amiri Baraka), Ted Joans, Walter DeLegall, and Percy Johnston. I kept Diane di Prima for myself because she was a woman with fire and myth in her mouth. Then, somebody told me worshipping others leads to mediocrity. So I stopped looking for roots and heroes and heroines and I found my peers, Pedro Pietri, Felipe Luciano, Gylan Kain, Etnairis Rivera, Sonia Sanchez, Jessica Hagedorn, Jan Mirikitani, and Thulani Davis, poets I could work with and be inspired by on a weekly if not daily basis. Later I'd add Susan Griffin, Judy Grahn, Alta, and Leslie Marmon Silko, Joy Harjo, Alurista, and Jimmy Santiago Baca to my list of influences, healers, and friends. Language is for me like the nectar of the living, I find it singing to me everywhere I go. I dance with Dianne McIntyre, Eleo Pomare, Mickey Davidson, Dyane Harvey, Idris Ackamoor, and Cecil Taylor whenever I hear my folks speak. No, I didn't forget Alice Walker, Toni Morrison, and Zora Neale Hurston. I just figured, you could figure that out about me on your own.

a history: *for colored girls who have considered suicide/ when the rainbow is enuf*

for colored girls who have considered suicide/ when the rainbow is enuf was first presented at the Bacchanal, a women's bar just outside Berkeley, California. With Paula Moss & Elvia Marta, who worked with me in Raymond Sawyer's Afro-American dance company & Halifu's The Spirit of Dance; Nashira Ntosha, a guitarist and program coordinator at KP00-FM (one of the few Bay Area stations focusing on women's programming); Jessica Hagedorn, a poet & reading tour companion; & Joanna Griffin, co-founder of the Bacchanal, publisher of Effie's Press, & a poet. We just did it. Working in bars waz a circumstantial aesthetic of poetry in San Francisco from Spec's, an old beat hangout, to "new" Malvina's, Minnie's Can-Do Club, the Coffee Gallery, & the Rippletad. With as much space as a small studio on the Lower East Side, the five of us, five women, proceeded to dance, make poems, make music, make a woman's theater for about twenty patrons. This was December of 1974. We were a little raw, self-conscious, & eager. Whatever we were discovering in ourselves that nite had been in progress among us for almost two years.

I first met Jessica & Nashira thru Third World Communications (the Women's Collective) when the first anthology of Third World women writers in the U.S.A. was published. With Janice Mirikitani, Avotcja, Carol Lee Sanchez, Janet Campbell Hale, Kitty Tsui, Janice Cobb, Thulani, and a score more, San Francisco waz inundated with women poets, women's readings, & a multi-lingual woman presence, new to all of us & desperately appreciated. The force of these readings on all of us waz to become evident as we directed our energies toward clarifying our lives—& the lives of our mothers, daughters, & grandmothers— as women. During the same period, Shameless Hussy Press & the Oakland Women's Press Collective were also reading anywhere & everywhere they could. In a single season, Susan Griffin, Judy Grahn, Barbara Gravelle, & Alta were promoting the poetry & presence of women in a legendary male-poet's environment. This is the energy & part of the style that nurtured *for colored girls* . . .

More stable as a source of inspiration & historical continuity waz the Women's Studies Program at Sonoma State College, where i worked with J. J. Wilson, Joanna Griffin, & Wopo Holup over a three-year span. Courses designed to make women's lives & dynamics familiar to us—such as: Woman as Artist; Woman as Poet; Androgynous Myths in Literature; Women's Biography I & II; Third World Women Writers—are inextricably bound to the development of my sense of the world, myself, & the women's language. Studying the mythology of women from antiquity to present day led directly to the piece *Sechita* in which a dance hall girl is perceived as deity, as slut, as innocent & knowing. Unearthing the mislaid, forgotten, &/or misunderstood woman writers, painters, mothers, cowgirls, & union leaders of our pasts proved to be both a supportive experience & a challenge not to let them down, not to do less than—at all costs not to be less woman than—our mothers, from Isis to Marie Laurencin, Zora Neale Hurston to Käthe Kollwitz, Anna May Wong to Calamity Jane.

Such joy & excitement I knew in Sonoma, then I would commute back the sixty miles to San Francisco to study dance with Raymond Sawyer, Ed Mock, & Halifu. Knowing a woman's mind & spirit had been allowed me, with dance I discovered my body more intimately than I had imagined possible. With the acceptance of the ethnicity of my thighs & backside came a clearer understanding of my voice as a woman & as a poet. The freedom to move in space, to demand of my own sweat a perfection that could continually be approached, though never known, waz poem to me, my body & mind ellipsing, possibly for the first time in my life. Just as Women's Studies had rooted me to an articulated female heritage & imperative, so dance as explicated by Raymond Sawyer & Ed Mock insisted that everything African, everything halfway colloquial, a grimace, a strut, an arched back over a yawn, waz mine. I moved what waz my unconscious knowledge of being in a colored woman's body to my known everydayness. The depth of my past waz made tangible to me in Sawyer's *Ananse,* a dance exploring the Diaspora to contemporary Senegalese music, pulling ancient trampled spirits out of present-tense Afro-American dance. Watching Ed Mock re-create the Step Brothers' or Bert Williams's routines in class or on the stage, in blackface mimicking Eddie Cantor or Gloria Swanson, being the rush of irony & control that are the foundation of jazz dance, was as startling as humbling. With Raymond Sawyer & Ed Mock, Paula Moss & I learned the wealth of our bodies, if we worked, if we opened up, if we made the dance our own.

The first experience of women's theater for me as a performer waz the months I spent with Halifu Osumare's The Spirit of Dance, a troupe of five to six black women who depicted the history of black dance from its origins in Western Africa thru to the popular dances seen on our streets. Without a premeditated or conscious desire to create a female piece, that's what, in fact, Halifu did. Working in San Francisco & Berkeley public schools as an adjunct to Ethnic Studies, I learned the mechanics of self-production & absorbed some of Halifu's confidence in her work, the legitimacy of our visions. After some 73 performances with The Spirit of Dance, I left the company to begin production of *for colored girls...*

In the summer of 1974 I had begun a series of seven poems, modeled on Judy Grahn's *The Common Woman,* which were to explore the realities of seven different kinds of women. They were numbered pieces: the women were to be nameless & assume hegemony as dictated by the fullness of their lives. The first of the series is the poem *one* (orange butterflies & aqua sequins), which prompted the title & *this is for colored girls who have considered suicide/ when the rainbow is enuf.* I waz smitten by my own language, & called all the performances I waz to give from then on by that title. In other words, all the readings & choreopoetry that Paula Moss & I developed after that summer waz *for colored girls...* We started at the Bacchanal & worked through the winter at Ed Mock's dance studio with the assistance of West Coast Dance Works, setting pieces & cleaning up poems. I found two bands, the Sound Clinic (a horn trio) & Jean Desarmes & his Reggae Blues Band, who agreed to work with us if I found space & I did. The space we used waz the space I knew: Women's Studies departments, bars, cafés, & poetry centers. With the selection of poems changing, dependent upon our audience & our mood, & the dance growing to take space of its own, so that Paula inspired my words to fall from me with her body, & the Sound Clinic working with new arrangements of Ornette Coleman compositions & their own, & the Reggae Blues Band giving Caribbean renditions of Jimi Hendrix & Redding, we set dates for Minnie's Can-Do Club in Haight-Ashbury. The poets showed up for us, the dancers showed up for us, the women's community showed up, & we were listed as a "must see" in the *Bay Guardian*. Eight days after our last weekend at Minnie's, Paula & I left to drive cross-country to New York to do "the show," as we called it, at the Studio Rivbea in New York.

Our work in San Francisco waz over. With the courage of children, we staged the same sort of informal & improvised choreopoems at Rivbea during the Summer Music Festival. Instead of the Standing-Room-Only crowds we were accustomed to in San Francisco, my family & a few friends came to see our great project. One of these friends, Oz Scott, & my sister Ifa Iyaun, who were instrumental in the development of *for colored girls . . . ,* saw the show that night. Oz offered to help me with the staging of the work for a New York audience, since Paula & I obviously didn't understand some things. We moved from the Rivbea to the Old Reliable on East 3rd Street to work through some of the ideas Oz had & the new things Paula & I were developing. Gylan Kain of the Original Last Poets waz working there every Monday night. We worked with him & any other poets & dancers who showed up. Several members of the original New York show came to us just this haphazardly. Aku Kadogo & I both had scholarships at Dianne McIntyre's Sounds in Motion dance studio. I asked her if she felt like improvising on the Lower East Side, she agreed & has been with the show ever since. Laurie Carlos stopped by one evening. She stayed. Somehow word got out & people started coming to the back room of this neighborhood bar. We moved to a new bar down the street, DeMonte's, after eleven weeks of no-pay hard-work three sets a night—maybe a shot of cognac on the house.

The show at DeMonte's waz prophetic. By this time, December of 1975, we had weaned the piece of extraneous theatricality, enlisted Trazana Beverley, Laurie Carlos, Laurie Hayes, & Aku Kadogo, & of course, Paula & I were right there. The most prescient change in the concept of the work waz that I gave up directorial powers to Oz Scott. By doing this, I acknowledged that the poems & the dance worked on their own to do & be what they were. As opposed to viewing the pieces as poems, I came to understand these twenty-odd poems as a single statement, a choreopoem.

We finally hit at DeMonte's. Those institutions I had shunned as a poet—producers, theaters, actresses, & sets—now were essential to us. *for colored girls who have considered suicide/ when the rainbow is enuf* waz a theater piece. Woodie King picked up our option to produce us as a Workshop under Equity's Showcase Code at Henry Street. With the assistance of the New York Shakespeare Festival & Joe Papp, we received space & a set, lights, & a mailing list, things Paula & I had done without for two years. We opened at Henry Street with two new actress-dancers, Thea Martinez & Judy Dearing. Lines of folks & talk all over the black & Latin community propelled us to the Public Theater in June. Then to the Booth Theater on Broadway in September of 1976.

Every move we've made since the first showing of *for colored girls . . .* in California has demanded changes of text, personnel,

& staging. The final production at the Booth is as close to distilled as any of us in all our art forms can make it. With two new actresses, Janet League & Risë Collins, & with the help of Seret Scott, Michele Shay, & Roxanne Reese, the rest of the cast is enveloping almost 6,000 people a week in the words of a young black girl's growing up, her triumphs & errors, our struggle to become all that is forbidden by our environment, all that is forfeited by our gender, all that we have forgotten.

I had never imagined not doing *for colored girls* . . . It waz just my poems, any poems I happened to have. Now I have left the show on Broadway, to write poems, stories, plays, my dreams. *for colored girls* . . . is either too big for my off-off-Broadway taste, or too little for my exaggerated sense of freedom, held over from seven years of improvised poetry readings. Or, perhaps, the series has actually finished itself. Poems come on their own time: i am offering these to you as what i've received from this world so far.

> *i am on the other side of the rainbow/ picking up pieces of*
> *days spent waitin for the poem to be heard/ while you listen/*
> *i have other work to do/*

unrecovered losses/ black theater traditions

as a poet in american theater/ i find most activity that takes place on our stages overwhelmingly shallow/ stilted & imitative. that is probably one of the reasons i insist on calling myself a poet or writer/ rather than a playwright/ i am interested solely in the poetry of a moment/ the emotional & aesthetic impact of a character or a line. for too long now afro-americans in theater have been duped by the same artificial aesthetics that plague our white counterparts/ "the perfect play," as we know it to be/ a truly european framework for european psychology/ cannot function efficiently for those of us from this hemisphere.

furthermore/ with the advent of at least 6 musicals about the lives of black musicians & singers/ (*Eubie, Bubbling Brown Sugar, Ain't Misbehavin', Mahalia*, etc.)/ the lives of millions of black people who dont sing and dance for a living/ are left un-attended to in our theatrical literature. not that the lives of Eu-bie Blake or Fats Waller are well served in productions lacking any significant book/ but if the lives of our geniuses arent art-fully rendered/ & the lives of our regular & precious are ignored/ we have a double loss to reckon with.

if we are drawn for a number of reasons/ to the lives & times of black people who conquered their environments/ or at least their pain/ with their art, & if these people are mostly musi-cians & singers & dancers/ then what is a writer to do to draw the most from human & revealing moments from lives spent in nonverbal activity. first of all we should reconsider our choices/ we are centering ourselves around these artists for what reasons/ because their lives were richer than ours. because they did something white people are still having a hard time duplicat-ing/ because they proved something to the world like Jesse Owens did/ like Billie Holiday did. i think/ all the above contribute to the proliferation of musicals abt our musicians/ without forcing us to confront the real implications of the dy-namic itself. we are compelled to examine these giants in order to give ourselves what we think they gave the worlds they lived in/ which is an independently created afro-american aesthetic. but we are going abt this process backwards/ by isolating the art forms & assuming a very narrow perspective vis-à-vis our own history.

if Fats Waller & Eubie Blake & Charlie Parker & Syvilla Fort & Katherine Dunham moved the world outta their way/ how did they do it/ certainly not by mimicking the weakest arena in american art/ the american theater. we must move our theater into the drama of our lives/ which is what the artists we keep resurrecting (or allowing others to resurrect) did in the first place/ the music & dance of our renowned predecessors appeals to us because it directly related to the lives of those then living & the lives of the art forms.

in other words/ we are selling ourselves & our legacy quite cheaply/ since we are trying to make our primary statements with somebody else's life/ and somebody else's idea of what theater is. i wd suggest that: we demolish the notion of straight theater for a decade or so, refuse to allow playwrights to work without dancers & musicians. "coon shows" were somebody else's idea. we have integrated the notion that serious drama must be words/ with no music & no dance/ cuz that wd take away the seriousness of the event/ cuz we all remember too well/ the chuckles & scoffs at the notion that all niggers cd sing & dance/ & most of us can sing & dance/ & the reason that so many plays written to silence & stasis fail/ is cuz most black people have some music and movement in our lives. we do sing & dance. this is a cultural reality. this is why i find the most inspiring theater among us to be in the realms of music & dance.

i think of my collaboration with David Murray on *A Photograph*/ & on *Where the Mississippi Meets the Amazon*/ & on *Spell #7*/ in which music functions as another character. Teddy & His Sizzling Romancers (David Murray, sax; Anthony Davis, piano; Fred Hopkins, bass; Paul Maddox, drums; Michael Gregory Jackson, guitar, harmonica, & vocals) were as important as the Satin Sisters/ though the thirties motif served as a vehicle to introduce the dilemmas of our times. in *A Photograph* the cello (Abdul Wadud) & synthesizer (Michael Gregory Jackson) solos/ allowed Sean to break into parts of himself that wd have been unavailable had he been unable to "hear." one of the bounties of black culture is our ability to "hear"/ if we were to throw this away in search of less (just language) we wd be damning ourselves. in slave narratives there are numerous references to instruments/ specifically violins, fifes, & flutes/ "talking" to the folks. when working with Oliver Lake (sax) or Baikida Carroll (trumpet) in *From Okra to Greens/* or Jay Haggard (vibes) in *Five Nose Rings & Soweto Suite/* i am terribly aware of a conversation. in the company of Dianne McIntyre/ or of Dyane Harvey's work with the Eleo Pomare Dance Company/ one is continually aroused by the immediacy of their movements/ "do this movement like yr life depends on it" as McIntyre says.

the fact that we are an interdisciplinary culture/ that we understand more than verbal communication/ lays a weight on afro-american writers that few others are lucky enough to have been born into. we can use with some skill virtually all our physical senses/ as writers committed to bringing the world as we remember it / imagine it/ & know it to be to the stage/ we must use everything we've got. i suggest that everyone shd cue from Julius Hemphill's wonderful persona, Roi Boye/ who ruminates & dances/ sings & plays a saxophone/ shd cue from Cecil Taylor & Dianne McIntyre's collaboration on *Shadows/* shd cue from Joseph Jarman & Don Moye (of the Art Ensemble of Chicago) who are able to move/ to speak/ to sing & dance & play a myriad of instruments in *Egwu-Anwu.* look at Malinke who is an actor/ look at Amina Myers/ Paula Moss/ Aku Kadogo/ Michele Shay/ Laurie Carlos/ Ifa Iyaun Bayeza, & myself in *Negress/* a collective piece which allowed singers, dancers, musicians, & writers to pass through the barriers & do more than 1 thing, dance to Hemphill or the B.A.G. (Black Artists Group)/ violinist Ramsey Ameen lets his instrument make his body dance & my poems shout. i find that our contemporaries who are musicians are exhibiting more courage than we as writers might like to admit.

in the first version of *Boogie Woogie Landscapes* i presented myself with the problem of having my person/ body, voice, & language/ address the space as if i were a band/ a dance company, & a theater group all at once. cuz a poet shd do that/ create an emotional environment/ felt architecture.

to paraphrase Lester Bowie/ on the night of the World Saxophone Quartet's (David Murray, Julius Hemphill, Hamiet Bluiett & Oliver Lake) performance at the Public Theater/ "those guys are the greatest comedy team since the Marx Brothers." in other words/ they are theater. theater which is an all-encompassing moment/ a moment of poetry/ the opportunity to make something happen. as writers we might think more often of the implications of an Ayler solo/ the meaning of a contradiction in anybody's body. we are responsible for saying how we feel. we "ourselves" are high art. our world is honesty & primal response.

my pen is a machete

although i rarely read reviews of my work/ two comments were repeated to me by "friends" for some reason/ & now that i am writing abt my own work/ i am finally finding some use for the appraisals of strangers. one new york critic had accused me of being too self-conscious of being a writer/ the other from the midwest had asserted that i waz so involved with the deconstruction of the english language/ that my writing approached verbal gymnastics like unto a reverse minstrel show. in reality, there is an element of truth in both ideas/ but the lady who thought i waz self-conscious of being a writer/ apparently waz never a blk child who knew that blk children didnt wear tiger skins n chase lions around trees n then eat pancakes/ she waznt a blk child who spoke an english that had evolved naturally/ only to hear a white man's version of blk speech that waz entirely made up & based on no linguistic system besides the language of racism. the man who thought i wrote with intentions of outdoing the white man in the acrobatic distortions of english was absolutely correct. i cant count the number of times i have viscerally wanted to attack deform n maim the language that i waz taught to hate myself in/ the language that perpetuates the notions that cause pain to every black child as s/he learns to speak of the world and the "self." yes/ being an afro-american writer is something to be self-conscious abt/ & yes/ in order to think n communicate the thoughts n feelings i want to think n communicate/ i haveta fix my tool to my needs/ i have to take it apart to the bone/ so that the malignancies/ fall away/ leaving us space to literally create our own image.

i have not ceased to be amazed when i hear members of an audience whispering to one another in the foyers of theaters/ that they had never imagined they cd feel so much for characters/ even though they were black (or colored/ or niggers, if they dont notice me eavesdropping). on the other hand/ i hear other members of an audience say that there were so many things in the piece that they had felt/ experienced/ but never had found words to express/ even privately/ to themselves. these two phenomena point to the same dilemma/ the straightjacket that the english language slips over the minds of all americans. there are some thoughts that black people just dont have/ according to popular mythology/ so white people never "imagine" we are having them/ & black people "block" vocabularies we perceive to be white folks ideas.* this will never do. for in addition to the obvious stress of racism n poverty/ afro-american culture/ in attempts to carry on/ to move forward/ has minimized its "emotional"

---

* Just examine *drylongso* by john langston gwaltney (random house, 1980).

vocabulary to the extent that admitting feelings of rage, defeat, frustration is virtually impossible outside a collective voice. so we can add self-inflicted repression to the cultural causes of our cultural disease of high blood pressure.

in everything i have ever written & everything i hope to write/ i have made use of what frantz fanon called "combat breath." although fanon waz referring to francophone colonies, the schema he draws is sadly familiar:

> There is no occupation of territory, on the one hand, and
> independence of persons on the other. It is the country as a
>   whole, its
> history, its daily pulsation that are contested, disfigured, in the
>   hope
> of final destruction. Under this condition, the individual's
>   breathing
> is an observed, an occupied breathing. It is a combat breathing.

fanon goes on to say that "combat breathing" is the living response/ the drive to reconcile the irreconcilable/ the black & white of what we live n where. (unfortunately, this language doesnt allow me to broaden "black" & "white" to figurative terms/ which is criminal since the words are so much larger n richer than our culture allows.) i have lived with this for 31 years/ as my people have lived with cut-off lives n limbs. the three pieces in this collection are the throes of pain n sensation experienced by my characters responding to the involuntary constrictions n amputations of their humanity/ in the context of combat breathing.

each of these pieces was excruciating to write/ for i had to confront/ again & again/ those moments that had left me with little

more than fury n homicidal desires. in *spell #7* i included a prologue of a minstrel show/ which made me cry the first times i
danced in it/ for the same reasons i had included it. the minstrel
may be "banned" as racist/ but the minstrel is more powerful in
his deformities than our alleged rejection of him/ for every night
we wd be grandly applauded. immediately thereafter/ we began to
unveil the "minstrels," who turned out to be as fun-loving as fey:

> *please/ let me join you/ i come all the way from brooklyn/ to*
> *   have a*
> *good time/ ya dont think I'm high do ya/ cd i please join ya. i just*
> *wanna have a good ol time.*

as contorted as sue-jean:

> *& i lay in the corner laughin/ with my drawers/ twisted*
> *   round my*
> *ankles & my hair standin every which way/ i waz laughin/*
> *   knowin i*
> *wd have this child/ myself/ & no one wd ever claim him/ cept*
> *   me/ cuz*
> *i was a low-down thing/ layin in sawdust & whiskey stains/*
> *   i laughed*
> *& had a good time masturbatin in the shadows.*

as angry as the actor who confides:

> *i just want to find out why no one has even been able to sound a*
> *gong & all the reporters recite that the gong is ringin/ while*
> *   we watch*
> *all the white people/ immigrants & invaders/ conquistadors &*

relatives of london debtors from georgia/ kneel & apologize
    to us/ just
for three or four minutes. now/ this is not impossible.

& after all that/ our true visions & rigors laid bare/ down from
the ceiling comes the huge minstrel face/ laughing at all of us
for having been so game/ we believed we cd escape his powers/
how naïve cd we be/ the magician explains:

  crackers are born with the right to be alive/
  i'm making ours right up here in yr face

the most frequently overheard comment abt *spell #7* when it
first opened at the public theater/ waz that it waz too intense. the
cast & i usedta laugh. if this one hour n 45 waz too much/ how
in the world did these same people imagine the rest of our lives
were/ & wd they ever be able to handle that/ simply being alive
& black & feeling in this strange deceitful country. which brings
me to *boogie woogie landscapes/* totally devoted to the emotional
topology of a yang woman/ how she got to be the way she is/
how she sees where she is. here/ again/ in the prologue lies the
combat breath of layla/ but she's no all-american girl/ or is she?

  the lil black things/ pulled to her & whimpered lil black whys/
    "why
  did those white men make red of our house/ why did those
    white men
  want to blacken even the white doors of our house/ why make
    fire of
  our trees & our legs/ why make fire/ why laugh at us/ say go
    home/
  arent we home/ arent we home?"

she was raised to know nothing but black & white two-dimensional planes/ which is what racism allots every one of us unless we fight. she found solace in jesus & the american way/ though jonestown & *american bandstand* lay no claims to her:

> *shall i go to jonestown or the disco? i cd wear red sequins or a*
>   *burlap*
> *bag. maybe it doesnt matter/ paradise is fulla surprises/ & the*
>   *floor of*
> *the disco changes colors like special species of vipers . . .*

her lover/ her family/ her friends torment her/ calm her with the little they have left over from their own struggles to remain sane. everything in *boogie woogie landscapes* is the voice of lay-la's unconscious/ her unspeakable realities/ for no self-respecting afro-american girl wd reveal so much of herself of her own will/ there is too much anger to handle assuredly/ too much pain to keep on truckin/ less ya bury it.

both *spell #7* & *boogie woogie landscapes* have elements of magic or leaps of faith/ in typical afro-american fashion/ not only will the lord find a way/ but there *is* a way outta here. this is the litany from the spirituals to jimi hendrix' "there must be some kinda way outta here"/ acceptance of my combat breath hasnt closed the possibilities of hope to me/ the soothing actualities of music n sorcery/ but that's why I'm doubly proud of *a photograph: lovers in motion*/ which has no cures for our "condition" save those we afford ourselves. the characters michael/ sean/ claire/ nevada/ earl/ are afflicted with the kinds of insecurities & delusions only available to those who learned themselves thru the traumas of racism. what is fascinating is the multiplicity of individual responses to this kind of oppression. michael displays her anger to her lovers:

I've kept a lover who waznt all-american/ who didnt believe/
 wdnt
straighten up/ oh I've loved him in my own men/ sometimes
 hateful
sometimes subtle like high fog & sun/ but who i loved is yr not
believin. i loved yr bitterness & hankered after that space in you
where you are outta control where you cannot touch or you
 wd kill
me/ or somebody else who loved you. i never even saw a picture &
I've loved him all my life he is all my insanity & anyone
 who loves
me wd understand.

while nevada finds a nurtured protection from the same phenomenon:

 mama/ will be be handsome & strong/ maybe from memphis/
  an old
 family of freedmen/ one of them reconstruction senators for a
  great
 grandfather . . .

their particular distortions interfere with them receiving one
another as full persons:

 claire: *no no/ i want nevada to understand that i understand*
  that sean's a niggah/ & that's why he's never gonna be great
  or whatever you call it/ cuz he's a niggah & niggahs cant be
  nothing.
 nevada: *see/ earl/ she's totally claimed by her station/ she cant*
  imagine anyone growing thru the prison of poverty to be-
  come someone like sean.

claire: *sean aint nothin but a niggah nevada/ i didn't know*
    you liked niggahs.

such is the havoc created in the souls of people who arent supposed to exist. the malevolence/ the deceit/ & manipulation
exhibited by these five are simply reflections of the larger world
they inhabit/ but do not participate in:

sean: *contours of life unnoticed!*
michael: *unrealized & suspect . . . our form is one of a blud-*
    geoned thing/wrapped in rhinestones & gauze/ blood al-
    most sparkling/ a wildness lurks always . . . oppression/
    makes us love one another badly/ makes our breathing
    mangled/ while i am desperately trying to clear the air/ in
    the absence of extreme elegance/ madness can set right in
    like a burnin gauloise on japanese silk. though highly cul-
    tured. even the silk must ask how to burn up discreetly.

the arbitrary nature of life as an african-american has been heralded, bemoaned, denied, wisht away, and yet we are still here.
how could a people who have been accused of having no history, no culture, no art, no souls, no common sense or rational
capacity survive so long? there is a simple answer that becomes
complicated as we undo lies, half-truths, and ignorance. we're
here for very specific reasons, as one of my favorite characters in
betsy brown mr. jeff would say, "i sho' do like to grow things,
sho' do like to grow things," then coyly meander offstage, an al
green quiver to his affirmation of our relationship to the earth,
soil, what we can get to come from it.
    there was very little that was arbitrary in the initial phases
of the global trade of african slaves. we were taken to specific
places to cultivate specific crops in regions of the new world

that mimicked certain african terrain and climate. how do I know this? plantation owners, slave traders, and wives of said personages kept densely exacting diaries or day books of why an african who had been somewhere else was taken outta there to be here to do something he or she could do better than anyone else anybody heard of. take rice for instance.

a bit of manumission
> because i have been in Simón Bolívar's library, Dessalines' easy chair, and José Martí's bedroom i have no choice. Freedom is not a commodity, nor am i, nor any of my people.

takin' a solo/
a poetic possibility/
a poetic imperative

if i asked: is this james brown or clifford jordan? you wd know.
if i said: is this fletcher henderson's band or the blackbyrds. you
wd know. i say, pick one: ayler or coltrane. here's another: charlie parker or ben webster. most of you wd know. the tone. the
lyric. rhythm & cadence of the musician is a personal thing to
you. you listen & learn the particular flow of a particular
somebody.

    soon you'll say that's oliver lake, not julius hemphill. or that
cdnt be david murray, that's gotta be hamiet bluie. you cd go so
far as to say joseph jarman wd never play anything like that. or
even point ornate coleman out/ shd you see him in any where/ &
say . . . he is history.

    we can do this with any kinda horn . . . clarinets, saxophones, trumpets/ tell me what does "some day my prince will come"/ mean to you. that is not snow white or walt disney/ that is miles davis. some of us can even differentiate mongo santamaria from carlos "patato" valdés and ray barretto from pacheco. others can pick ron carter from a segue of mingus & hopkins & favors. we hear so well/ remember solos that were improvisations/ we are thoroughly smitten by the nature of the thing/ if we talk abt music.

you never doubt bessie smith's voice. i cd not say to you, that's chaka khan singin *empty bed blues*. not cuz chaka khan cant sing *empty bed blues*/ but cuz bessie smith sounds a certain way, her way. if tina turner stood right here next to me & simply said "yes" . . . we wd all know/ no matter how much i love her/ no matter what kinda wig-hat i decide to wear/ my "yes" will never be tina's "yes." and that's what i want to discuss with you this evening.

we, as a people, or as a literary cult, or a literary culture/ have not demanded singularity from our writers. we cd all sound the same, come from the same region, be the same gender, born the same year. & though none of the above is true, a black writer can get away with/ abscond & covet for him or herself/ the richness of his or her person/ long before a black musician or singer cd.

now why is this? we don't understand the beauty of language? that cant be true. according to dillard & smith we make up a good part of contemporary american/ on our own. cd it be we assume a collaboration with any blk writer/ who attempts to re-create blk english/ blk culture/ cuz that's ours/ we were there/ we know abt that/ & that poet/ that novelist/ that playwright/ happened to be there at the time/ when some other somebody, just like me/ waz sayin or doin/ exactly what i say & do/ that wd mean there is absolutely no acceptance of blk personal reality/ that if you are 17, female & black in the u.s.a./ you have one solitary voice/ though you number 3 million/ no nuance exists for you/ you have been sequestered in the monolith/ the common denominator as persona. what i am trying to get to is the notion that as a people we have so claimed "the word"/ we dont even pay attention to who is speakin. is this leroi jones:

> *who will know what I am and what I wanted*
> *beneath the maze of memories & attitudes that*
> *shape the reality of everything. Beneath the*
> *necessity of taking or the necessity for being angry*
> *and beneath the actual core of life we make*
> *reference to digging deep into some young woman,*
> *and listening to her come.*

or imamu baraka?

> *we do not need to be fucked with*
> *we can be quiet and think and love the silence*
> *we need to look at trees more closely*
> *we need to listen*

there's a difference/ in the syntax, imagery & rhythm & theme. who is this: bob kaufman, david henderson? or thulani or papoleto meléndez or me:

> *i seek a phone & let you have it*
> *what you see is what you get*
> *if you limit yrself—you lose*

that's the division of a realm boarded by bebop & one sunk in syllable/ where only language defines reality. we have poets who speak to you of elephants & avenues/ we have others who address themselves to worlds having no existence beyond the word. that's fine. we live all those places. but, if, as i believe, we dont know the voice of a writer, the way we know "oh . . . that's trane"/ something is very wrong. we are unfortunately/ sellin ourselves down the river again. now/ we awready know abt that/ if we go down river again/ just cuz we dont know or care to recognize our particularities/ wont nobody come/ cuz dont nobody care/ if you dont know yr poets as well as yr tenor horns.

you dont resist count basie cuz he's from red bank, new jersey. i never heard of anyone disparaging eric dolphy for being born & raised in los angeles/ nobody is mad at pacheco cuz he is from the dominican republic/ but i can tell you who is a poet from chicago/ i cd say that's some west coast stuff/ or some new york number/ & there will be a great noddin of heads & uh-huhs/ cuz we dont ask a poet to speak/ we want a poet to talk like an arena/ or like a fire station/ to be everywhere/ all at once/ even if we never been there/ but especially/ if weve never been there/ we expect a closed space/ not her space/ not a secret/ not a closed room/ but the town/ we assume the poet to be the voice of everywhere we are not/ as opposed to bein "everything we are" . . . though what authentic musical criticism of our artists that exists/ always allows them the space to be themselves. a. b. spellman did not write a book callt/ *bebop*. he wrote a book called/ *four lives in the bebop business*. in *black music*/ leroi jones demanded only that each apple core/ be singular/ be, in this case, himself/ though that had more to do with circumstance than sexism.

my basic premise is that poets address themselves to the same issues as musicians/ but that we give the musicians more space to run with/ more personal legitimacy than we give our writ-

ers: here is a series of poems & compositions that approach the
same themes/ if not the same themes they approach the same
energy levels/ if not the same energy levels/ they approach the
same rhythmic offensive: as/ sun ra's version of *take the a train*
/ ishmael reed:

> *i am a cowboy in the boat of ra*
> *vamoosed from the temple i bedded*
> *down with Isis, Lady of the Boogaloo, dove*
> *down deep in her horny stuck up her Wells*
> *Far-ago in daring midday get away.*
> *"start grabbing the blue"*
> *i said from atop my double crown.*

or take victor hernández cruz' *doing poetry*:

> *the poet sees & hears the world. & there are many*
>   *worlds.*
> *people live in different worlds/ got different bags*
> *humans talk/ dance & make noise/ a poet must*
>   *make poetry*
> *out of that/ or make poetry out of his mind/ which*
> *took form in the world*
> *words & music travel.*
> *god wd not make anything bad or dirty. some people*
> *make dirty things happen tho.*
> *i see what's in the world & sing it like a god.*

& give the rest to dolphy . . . there is no incongruence here. but
you wd know dolphy & maybe not hernández cruz. here/ compare leroi jones with himself as baraka:

seeing no one. not wanting anyone. but you all.
  i want now to have all your minds.
    want now, to be them.

here is another nuance of baraka: *beautiful black women:*

Beautiful black women, fail, they act. Stop them,
  raining.
They are so beautiful, we want them with us. Stop
  them, raining
Beautiful, stop raining, they fail. We fail them &
  their lips stick out perpetually, at our weakness.
Raining. Stop them.
Black queens, Ruby Dee weeps at the window,
  raining, being lost in her life,
being what we all will be, sentimental
bitter frustrated, deprived of her fullest light.
Beautiful black women, it is still raining in this
  terrible land.

as so often assumed by academicians, the work as leroi jones does not overshadow the work of imamu technically. now/ hear david murray's *flowers for albert* & know that sorrows or incantations may be as gentle as they are grieving/ as lyrical as they are abandoned to despair. here, clarence major: *reflex & bone structure:*

on the wall is an edward hopper painting of an
  all-night
diner. the loneliness kills me. they bury me
  in atlanta.
cora invited shirley maclaine & marcello

mastroianni to the funeral but they dont show. a lot
of colored writers send flowers.

here is gylan kain's *#33 lovesong* which fits perfectly with julius
hemphill's *hard blues:*

> *we make love in the burning tenement*
> *my knife*
> *upon yr womb*
> *fingers upon yr neck/ you scream*
> *black satin woman*
> *you are the boston strangler turned in upon yr self*
> *down in the endless shaft of stairs*
> *i am the black flute*
> *yr vulva lips refused to play.*

or compare bob kaufman's *song of the broken giraffe* with oliver
lake's *altoviolin* or roscoe mitchell's *nonaah:*

> *I continued to love despite all the traffic-light*
> *   difficulties.*
> *In most cases, a sane hermit will beat a good*
> *   big man.*
> *We waited in vain for the forest fire, but the bus*
> *   waz late.*
> *All night we baked the government into a big*
> *   mud pie.*
> *Not one century passed without Shakespeare calling*
> *   us dirty names.*
> *With all those syllables, we cdnt write a cheerful*
> *   death notice.*

The man said we cd have a birthday party, if we
*   surrendered.*
Their soldiers refused to wear evening gowns on
*   guard duty.*
Those men in the basement were former
*   breakfast-food salesmen.*
We had a choice of fantasies, but naturally we
*   were greedy . . .*
At the moment of truth we were dancing a minuet
*   & missed out.*

kaufman's voice is quite like muhal richard abrams' *1 & 4 plus 2 & 7.* we assume the tune or composition is the person/ is the reality the tune is/ we assume a poet has no grounding/ the poem can float in the air & belong to all of us so long as we deny the individuality of the word/ the specificity of language cd allow us so much more. i suggest that thulani davis is quite as inclusive as the art ensemble of chicago/ in *people in sorrow:*

with closed lips & knotted secrets/ choke
*   the speech/*
cut the throat/ cut the throat behind the veil
the rich phantasma. wanted not taken
the nightmare & the dream
if you ask for me/ i'm never there
i hide in the streets

until we believe in the singularity of our persons/ our spaces, language, & therefore craft, we will not be nurtured consciously/ our writers will come across it/ if they want. but we wont recognize it/ cuz like i said is that conyus?

the way of the new world is endless, imposing
     & present
there is a different reality that i cannot recognize
in the living nor dead; the earth is moist with them
& below the vastness of the backwater
lie drummed skinned boys collapsed in silence.

or jessica hagedorn?

sometimes you remind me of lady day
& i tell you sadness
the weariness in yr eyes/ the walk you have
kinda brave when you swing yr hips
sometimes serenity in yr eyes
& the love always.

i know you know the difference between elvin jones & tony williams? if you take us as seriously as you take a saxophone, maybe we'll have decades of poems you'll never forget.

we assume a musical solo is a personal statement/ we think the poet is speakin for the world/ there's something wrong there, a writer's first commitment is to the piece itself. how the words fall & leap/ or if they dawdle & sit down fannin themselves. writers are dealing with language, not politics. that comes later. so much later. to think abt the politics of a poem before we think about the poem is to put what is correct before the moment/ if the moment waz not correct/ it still waz/ we dont castigate ornette coleman for *lonely woman* nor do we chastise the del-vikings for singing abt love all the time/ we accept what they gave us/ cuz that's what they had & it waz good.

when i take my voice into a poem or a story/ i am trying

desperately to give you that/ i am not trying to give you a history of my family/ the struggle of black people all over the world or the fight goin on upstairs tween susie & matt/ i am giving you a moment/ like something that isnt coming back/ a something particularly itself/ like an alto solo in december in nashville in 1937.

as we demand to be heard/ we want you to hear us. we come to you the way leroy jenkins comes or cecil taylor. or b. b. king. we come to you alone/ in the theater/ in the story/ & the poem/ like with billie holiday or betty carter/ we shd give you a moment that cannot be re-created, a specificity that cannot be confused/ our language shd let you know who's talkin, what we're talkin abt & how we cant stop saying this to you. some urgency accompanies the text. something important is going on. we are speakin. reaching for yr person/ we cannot hold it/ we dont wanna sell it/ we give you ourselves/ if you listen/ pietri:

> we are gathered here today to say we are gathered
> here today because we are not gathered somewhere
> else to say we are gathered here today & not
> somewhere else we are gathered here today because
> this is somewhere else/ & because we are not
> gathered somewhere else to tell you differently.

if you listen/
you cd imagine us like music & make us yrs.

> we can be quiet & think & love the silence
> we need to look at trees more closely
> we need to listen.

how i moved anna fierling to the
southwest territories
or
my personal victory over the armies of
western civilization

one evening last winter as i cut & pasted the preliminary script of *spell #7* in the lobby of the Public Theater i noticed a great bustling & repressed hysteria in the air. i saw more white men than usual in tuxedoes & three-piece suits. there were lavishly clad women of all types & classes posing by stairwells & elevators of a building i worked in. i paid little attention until i saw what i thought waz a group of official people. in this case, Mr. Papp, Herman Badillo, someone who i thought waz the mayor, some other people i waz sure were undercover cops & Gail Merrifield. oh, i said. there is something going on. then i realized that i must be cutting & pasting away, while *Coriolanus* prepared to open. well, i said to myself. shd i stop my own work to go see a classic that has not been altered to fit the needs of my century or my people? shd i stop work on something i feel so tenderly & passionately abt in order to submit myself to the presence of critics who can only hear that Afro-Americans & Latinos have diction what is not the diction of white folks? why shd i do that, i said to myself, when i can stay here with my own characters who talk fine to me/ who talk to me abt what i care abt. oh/ i said. Zake. You are an educated Afro-American. you can't stay away from Shakespeare on those grounds. you are trained to hear the lyric & wisdom of anything in the English language/ & Shakespeare/ well you were certainly exposed to Shakespeare. But an anglophile i am not.

the compromise. finish the script for *spell #7* that wd make up for any racial slights or abuses I endured in the audience. out of respect for the actors & Shakespeare i wd catch the second act & return another day to see the first act. after all/ I'd read *Coriolanus* when i waz 15 years old/ there waz no urgency abt all this.

yet that waznt true at all & i knew it. the urgency existed because of the vicious racist & virtually colonial attitudes expressed in the critical responses to *Julius Caesar,* the first production of the black & latin Shakespeare company that Mr. Papp had formed in the fall of 1978. not since Governor Faubus & good old George Wallace standing in the schoolhouse doorway had i read such indictments of the capacity of nonwhite people.

i had & still grapple with the idea of classics in the lives & arts of third world people. we have so much to do, so much to unearth abt our varied realities/ on what grounds do we spend our talents, hundreds of thousands of dollars, unknown quantities of time, to re-create experiences that are not our own?

does a colonial relationship to a culture/ in this case Anglo-Saxon imperialism/ produce a symbiotic relationship or a parasitic one? if we perform the classics/ giving our culture some leeway in an adaptation/ which is the parasite? why aren't the talents & perspectives of contemporary third world artists touted in the same grand fashion successful revivals of dead white artists are? all these things bothered me during the second act of *Coriolanus* but not so much that i wasn't moved to tears simply by the overwhelming power of the company/ i loved looking at them/ hearing them. i waz thoroughly committed to seeing more black, latin & asian artists addressing issues of the world. one thing that doing classics allows us/ that is such a relief/ is to do an evening of dialogue without having to restrict ourselves to the pains & myopia of racism in America. the power of white folks as we know it poses no boundaries in *Coriolanus* or *Julius Caesar*. they are not in it and hold no power—what escapism. the failure of the black and latin Shakespeare company is directly related to the actual power of white folks & the impotence that that sort of power brings. this impotence is an inability on the part of white audiences, critics, academicians & their specific mythologies of white supremacy to identify with black & latin actors as nobility. for in our hemisphere race & class are implacably engaged & it is a duel to the death. it resulted in the death of the black & latin Shakespeare company.

i cd feel as i clapped & shouted during curtain calls that it waz only the black folks who were clapping & shouting. the white people in the audience seemed more amazed that the black people had understood Shakespeare/ or that it waz possible to enjoy an entire evening when not a nigger danced/ let alone sang. i waz filled with an uncomfortable blend of excitement abt the actors, distain for the audience, anger that we had to do this at all, & satisfaction that we had. i went to have a drink, to think, to talk to somebody abt the mess of my fortune to be born black & Engligh-speaking.

at Lady Astor's i waited for the actors to congratulate them i thought/ or to commiserate/ cuz Ira Aldridge had done this 200 years before. cuz wasn't *Native Son* a classic/ cuz there waz nothing to combat the irrationality of racism that assaulted such benign adaptations as *Carmen Jones, The Wiz,* & *Medea.* i was angry/ for didn't i have a right to see my own kind do whatever the hell they liked? if i had had to struggle to identify with Anna Karenina & Blanche DuBois/ why cdnt white folks learn that skill/ that great leap of imagination that lets another person of another color become oneself. i began to list all the "white" shows i shd have seen done by black people/ so the experience cd have been more personal/ not fraught with so many double-thinks & excuses. i began with Twain/ *Tom Sawyer* & *Huckleberry Finn.* the list grew to include *Cat on a Hot Tin Roof, Death of a Sales-man, Marat/Sade* & *Mother Courage.*

Oz Scott, the only director with whom i had worked at that time, came to pick up the script for *spell #7.* i realized that what i feared abt the classics had indeed happened to me. i had forgotten abt my own work & waz involved in fruitless combat with myself abt the works of dead white men. just what white folks want. the only recourse waz to quiet the antagonisms i waz experiencing/ once & for all. how? by making the demon (the classics) bend to my will. only by directly assaulting what i felt as an oppressive authority figure wd i free myself of the need to continually debate what i really understood to be a waste of time & energy. cuz my own life history revealed that no matter what i thought i waz doing/ the public perception had to do with that i waz a black person & what a miracle it must be for me to be articulate.

Oz & i decided on *Mother Courage.* this waz an arbitrary

decision based on mild intoxication & Brecht's more aristo-
cratic position in the company of Twain, O'Neill, & Miller. we
delighted in the obvious presumptuousness of two black people
assigning themselves the task of toying with one of Europe's
precious sons. i went around Lady Astor's with Oz speaking to
actors, black & white, abt my sudden respect for the classics &
how black people really must do one/ it's like having one's ped-
igree verified. some weeks later/ with no instigation from me/
Mr. Papp called to ask if i wd consider adapting *Mother Courage.* yes i said without hesitation. now i wd move what waz sacred to them/ to something sacred for me. manipulation of the
symbols is not unlike big game hunting: learning the habits,
expectations & reflexes of other animals allows us to slay them.
i wd have my chance to hunt the cherished words of dead white
men & using all my Afro-American reservoirs of magic, hate &
understanding of my people/ undo one myth & replace it with
my own.

while i've never been fond of anglophone literature, i've always respected German writers. i dont know why. my guess is
that i move toward that which is contrary to the traditions of
the language that i learned to hate myself in/ as a black person/
as part of the colonial bounty of empires built from the sweat
of my particular ancestors. with all the fallacies rampant in
that thought (think of Martinique, Curaçao, Brazil), my pen-
chant for German & French literature exists to this day. doing
Mother Courage wd permit me to pay homage & to defeat the
prophecies of Bertolt Brecht/ who i admired immensely at the
same time that i cd never trust/ cuz he was after all still white:
my admiration for Brecht is in the text of my adaptation and
the care i took not to betray him. but if a work is truly classic it
must function for other people in other times. i believe that
Brecht's work does this. his love of the complexity of ordinary

people/ his commitment to a better life for all of us/ his use of politics & passion/ music & monologues/ were not so different from my own approaches to theater. (i might have felt estranged had Mr. Papp asked me to adapt Chekhov, Artaud, or O'Neill.) i also knew that Brecht had much more artistic control of his work than i wd have of my adaptation. first because i cd not direct such a massive piece. second, because i had no Paul Dessau or Kurt Weill of my own to produce the sounds of the Reconstruction as i heard them. in this way, my Brechtian adaptation waz inordinately non-Brechtian. nevertheless, the text left me plenty of room to exert my powers.

Mother Courage has most to do/ at least from my vantage point/ with the actual responsibilities all of us must accept for the machinations of the capitalist state. the history of Afro-Americans is so mired in the sluggish imaginations of racism that our true experiences in the development of this country are looked upon as quirks. how in the hell could the 14 million blacks freed after the Civil War have an insignificant relationship to Manifest Destiny, to miscegenation, the franchise, the life of a nation moved by dreams of empire & subjugation of nature from sea to shining sea? that's where my *Mother Courage* begins/ with the first thirty years of struggle by the first mass of freed slaves to become American. the first thirty years of our culpability in the genocidal activities of the cavalry, the exploitation of non-English-speaking peoples, the acceptance of the primacy of the dollar. if i must come to terms with being a descendant of imperialist assimilationists who were willing if not eager to murder & destroy other people of color in the name of a flag that represents only white folks, then let me use a vehicle conceived in the heartland of one of history's most cruel ideologies, Nazism. being Afro-American does not exclude our participation in the hoax of the myths of the western pioneers, nor does the fact that we are black disavow the courage of those pioneers who were willing to fight the land, their better judgment & the never-ending viciousness of racists with no more than Jesus & a shotgun.

i now have no further need to experience intimately the thought processes of a great white dead writer/ in the way i lived Brecht's conscious mind for six months. *Mother Courage* gave me the opportunity to ground myself in the history of my people in this land. i can offer this version of Brecht's masterpiece as the adventures & trials of people of color of the last century in a language of my own. now i have colored wagon trains & towns, black conquistadores & hoodlums, wenches & ladies of refinement embedded in the soils & myths i waz raised on, but excluded from.

I have no need to deride or defend the social experiment of third world companies dedicated to the classics/ i have resolved the conflicts for myself. i owe not one more moment of thought to the status of European masters. i don't have to worry that Ira Aldridge thinks poorly of me for not accepting a challenge/ the battle is over. i am settling my lands with my characters, my language, my sense of right & wrong, my sense of time & rhythm. the rest of my life can go on along in relative aesthetic peace/ the enemy has been banished from my horizons. as the magician in *spell #7* said: "crackers are born with the right to be alive/ I'm making mine up right here in yr face/ why dontcha go on ahead & push me."

getting where i haveta be/
the nature of collaboration in recent works

AT THE EARLY SPRING BLACK THEATER SUMMIT "ON Golden Pond" convened by August Wilson, William Cook, and Victor Leo Walker II, there were rousin' discussions of the differences/aesthetic antagonisms between theater arts and performance art. Having been in the process of developing a performance piece, sought to remove the mystery, the condescension, and confusion surrounding this art form to which I continually return, after a novel, after the essay, after the play. I find myself a nurturing home in what for me is my experience of performance art.

I started out two decades ago as a performing poet known to work frequently with dancers and musicians. This was not a new thing. Think Isadora Duncan, Kerouac, Baraka. The Art Ensemble of Chicago. What was new was my entire evening's oeuvre was designed to invoke fully the power of movement and sound to the extent that the implications and nuances of the language would hopefully fly from my control & to that of my collaborators who would finish a thought, or a feeling state, with movement or sound. So, in my case, precisely as in traditional theater, everyone's efforts are directed toward the exploration and integrity of the text. The difference being that the text grows; sometimes, specific musical compositions or choreography become essential to the dynamic. In other words, while the poem/monologue can stand on its own, another parallel evolution of the same piece requires music and movement as involved in the poem/monologues' rhythms, metaphors, and images as breath itself. These elements must be "discovered."

Just in the past few days a musician's representative asked me what song this fella should have ready for a short performance in the East. Well, I had to tell her that if he needed "songs" and for me to pick them, that I was virtually certain nothing would come of our working together, but thanks anyway. How did I know to do this with only ten days to go? It was very simple. If the piece to be performed is based on the "text," then that's what the possible collaborator should have asked for. I do not use background music, but rather music that pushes a piece to be more than what it already is, to help redefine the implications of the words, the syllables, themselves. In fact, at one time I had a group called Syllable with John Purcell (reeds) and Jean-Paul Bourelly (guitars-percussion). Our rehearsals were very different from straight theater rehearsals, in the sense that we had to stop and start for new ideas of what could go between words, phrases, rhythmic or lyrical passages that could be extended, made more powerful, where the words were achin' to become non-verbal flights, i.e., solos. Were the "bridges" in the musical sense somewhere in the language that we could put a "hook" on? All this has to be done with someone in such control of his/her craft that leaving space in another art form doesn't intimidate or throw them. I've worked (only once/one chance) with dancers who actually thought they could "set" a 12-measure improvisation every other couplet, & that I wouldn't catch on. Humph.

Lucky for me my closely nurtured and shared dance experience with the likes of Mickey Davidson, Dianne McIntyre and Dyane Harvey, and I need mention Paula Moss (*fog*) who gave movement vocabulary that allowed our varied instincts to take off from one another. The same holds true for the work I do with Kahil El'Zabar, Joe & Lester Bowie, Olu Dara, and Chico Freeman. They know my work. I know their work to the extent that I met Joe Bowie, the leader for Defunkt outside the Smithsonian just before a "standard" poetry event. within a half hour, and in one improvisation, Joe and I were onstage like Butterbeans & Susie. the same thing happened at the Atlanta Black Arts Festival '96, when I was able to spontaneously enlist Olu Dara in my presentation, knowing his capacity on acoustic guitar, his ability to write and his timing, plus familiarity with the genesis and evolution of my work, would allow for secure public exploration and expansions of the texts.

On the other hand, pieces like *Liliane*, directed and choreographed by Mickey Davidson and produced by Walter Dallas' Freedom Theater and Rick Kahn's Crossroads Theater, required improvisational charting, as well as immersion of new people (dancers and musicians) who'd never been given full responsibility for their contribution to the work as integrals. There are no "side-men" in this work, no one who has to be "told" what's going on or what to do. Even, when Freeman, Harey, and I worked on Sonnet #128 for the Acting Company's production *Love's Fires*, we listened, read, played with their piece through e-mail, videos and telephone. the give and take are endless, the pieces are never exactly the same each time. I do not intend for them to be. While working with El'Zabar on *Ellington is Not a Street*, performed in Idris Ackamoor's New Performance in Black Theatre Series at Larry Leon Hamlin's National Black Theatre Festival '97, we sent videos and cassettes back and forth from Chicago to Houston, until we felt sure we'd created a foundation pliable enough for us to respond to unexpected "moments" created onstage and demanding further interpretation; in addition to propelling the possible movements suggested by Mickey Davidson's movement patterns, which gave us the theatrical stability to work with a lighting designer. I didn't know whether a word, note or a movement would get where I had to go, but I knew I'd be there.

That's how I do what I do.

ii.

why i had to dance//

one/
when i was a small child/ colored as i am/ my favorite movies
were busby berkeley musicals with that magnificent choreogra-
phy/ much of which i later learned was due to his innovative use
of cinematography/ the women blonde and buxom/ one after
another on spirals of staircases, or piano keys/ or neath the arcs
of feathers or men's arms/ dazzled me/ i knew my life was to be
that of a chorus girl or a psychiatrist/ how did i jump over the
fact of their whiteness and my very brown-ness/ it was very
simple/ i made everybody on stage 'colored'/ i changed the facts/
so to speak/ i knew /'Negro' women were beautiful/ could dance/
and manage headdresses/ i also knew we were already associated
with the exotic/ how did i know these things?

my mother//

my mother was not only blonde at that time/ but she could dance/ and carried herself with aplomb and a flirtatiousness which was at the core of the berkeley chorus girl/ then/ too/ my parents danced a lot/ not unlike the last big hit by luther vandross/ i watched my father dance with my mother again and again/ & every time they went some where/ like cuba or haiti/ they came back not only with instruments/ but with new dances that apparently had ties with the colored people/ that was the beginning of the foundation of my pan-afro-hemispheric consciousness/ wherever the colored people were/ there were dances i could do & claim as mine/ cause/ i was colored too.

my mother and her friends were living examples of beauti-ful/ black women/ with their handsome male partners/ dancin' in the kitchen/ on the landings of the stairways and tween the french doors long into the night/ nothin was impossible/ cause I'd see the katherine dunham dancers in *stormy weather* and the nicholas brothers numerous times/ leapin' over one another's heads to splits and back up again in the complex rhythms of their taps/ each year i looked for carmen de lavalade in *ahmal and the night visitors* on television and an occasional appear-ance by maria tallchief/ the native american prima ballerina close to my heart/ cuz we were not only colored but lumbee/ cherokee and blackfoot/ the westerns of the day were embar-rassing/ they lacked for form/ the so-called savages/ i knew had form/ we all did/ it was in the drums/ drums letting us know what to do// later in nigerian dance classes i learned this was in fact the truth/ so many convictions i developed as a youngster turned out to be actualities as a serious adult student of african, caribbean and modern dance/ to have had the favor of the spirits

all these years to have a continuity of an aesthetic that is at the
heart of blackness//
    my mother//

    my grandmother describing cakewalks at dances in charleston/
       my mother and my grandmother blushing as my aunt
       emma demonstrated the "shimmy"/ always could shake
    that thang/ aunt emma/ they all said i take after her/ emma
    maybe great aunt marie doin the charleston/ in charleston
    dance frees the soul/ one generation/ to the next//

    i remember ruby keeler in *42nd street* so dark/ so darin in
       her tap solos/
    movin from chorus girl to star/ precedent set.

    my mother//

    the masonic hall/ my sister & i runnin to ballet & tap dance
       classes/
    not far away from the train station/ on to broadway to/ new
       york or/ the south
    so many black people to the south/ the richness there//
    no one to look at my colored body as a predicament to get
       myself/
    out of/ my colored behind and thighs/ not to be used/ but
       escaped/
    till st. louis & the mississippi freed me like so many

    my mother//

    mama found a brown man to teach a bunch of us ballroom
       dance/ the way the negro

people do it/ the way she and daddy graced the kitchen
  landings/ there was
romance/ fronta the children/ fine examples of continuing
  courtship/
conga drums in the corner/ 'long with bongos and claves/
  leadin
eventually to the mississippi delta/ ridin the voice of tina
  turner/
or the ikettes/ once again/ a chorus girl/ even chuck berry
  had dancers

my mother//

threw parties/ found movements/ i learned from the top of
  the stairs/ the
spying of colored children on dances/ on domestic disputes
  at the dairy queen/
outside patients' houses/ outside the emergency room of
  saint mary's hospital/
all this katherine dunham & pearl primus captured in their
  choreography/

my mother//

ever seeking explanations/ demonstrations of our lives as
  "the negro"/
thru art she said/ and sought out syvilla fort/ then when we
  discovered my aunt britt/
grandma had disowned/ in trinidad/ steel drums/ graced
  our doorway/ &
i found there really were headdresses and sequins for a girl
  like me

it's in the blood
my mother say/
in the blood and practice//

few people knew at the time/ that the Revolutionary Action
     Movement/ RAM/ led by
robert williams was also/ associated with santeria/
many strategic decisions were made according to the
     readings of the madrinas and
padrinos of different houses/ we could drive all the way
     from boston to the bronx/ for
bembes for various santos or orishas/ there i learned many
     traditional dances/
oshun gazing at herself with her mirror/
shango with his lightning/
ogun with his ax/
elegua limping/
obatala with his hand on his hip and crumpled forward/
later i studied these dances in formal classes/ but without
     the sacred bata drums/ rarely did
we reach the fever pitches of the bembes themselves/ though
     we did reach higher planes
of consciousness/ this i believe/ cause where the music is
     climbing to heretofore unheard
levels of spirituality/ so too does dance/ & whether it was in
     the east deep in brooklyn or
clark center in mid-town manhattan/

black dance was alive with the spirit of the caribbean and
africa/ this was apparent at a once in a lifetime concert celebration for syvilla fort who along with ms. dunham had trained
most of the teachers i'd come in contact with or trained their

teachers/ at the majestic theater in one night/ i saw the best of what black dance new york had to offer/ from rod rodgers to chuck davis/ alvin ailey to dianne mcintyre/ everyone was there/ it was unbelievable/ i thought i had levitated/ but i made a serious commitment to study seriously that night/ i was standing with my sister/ ifa bayeza and bernadine jennings at the time/ that re-directed my life from the energy on the page to the energy and discipline of my body/ and the rhythm of my people//

when clark center was still at the Y at 51st and 8th ave/ titos sompa and a myriad of drummers taught congolese dance/ amazingly intricate steps and jumps with directional changes/ thelma hill ever steady and as my sister says "magical" teaching built muscle where there had been none and gave proper form to a mere diagonal walk/ we went no less than 4 times a week/ and held weekly poetry salons at our duplex in chelsea after glen brooks' afternoon lessons/ there was an energy in the air that was the buoy for all our black and latin nationalist focus/ we were going to make a difference/ not unlike rael lamb's solo eight/ rod rodgers when he slides forcefully across the main stage only to leap like a phoenix in the next breath/ after a very brief stint at the college of new jersey teaching poetry and folklore/ after one visit with etnairis rivera of old Young Lord's days one poetry readin and an airplane ticket away/ i was off to lone mountain college in san francisco for a three-week dance intensive with zak thomas/ this is a critical moment/ when i decided that dance was as important to me as writing/ that in order to write. i had to sweat/ to reach some sort of endorphin high to get to the truth/ which was the word/ this would change over time//

in terms of protocol everything that should not happen to get to a presentation of a dance piece/ happened/ the dancers were called enough names to cower in the corner/ while the stage manager was verbally and physically assaulted by the choreographer/ the floor covered with glass shards as the audience entered the theater/ the choreography calling all the female dancers to virtually peel grapes for the choreographer who was the center of the piece/ every element went awry/ but not to worry i met a stage door johnny who i found out later was on the fbi's top ten for trying to blow up the walter reed army hospital/ in my early adulthood/ politics and the arts were truly wed at the hip or thereabouts//

for instance/ the first annual national black power conference/ held in newark new jersey was opened by none other than olatunji and his dancers and the chuck davis dancers who inspired me beyond belief/ for these women who danced so powerfully were not balanchine-bodied dancers/ but big-boned wholesome women moving as if fairy dust was neath their feet/ to my mind that meant that our commitment to the movement meant that all our resources intellectual as well as physical had to be dedicated to the liberation movement/ which is one of the reasons i had to dance/

> to inspire consciousness in our people at all levels/
> my mother believed in the "race" as a cause/
> not a state of being/
> but a call to arms/ to the arts/ as champions or warriors
> daddy ran gyms for boxers/fighters
> they also raised one

in california where i decided to stay/ i found raymond sawyer's afro-asian dance company/ which felt more natural than i have ever felt in high school/ and has the tension for perfection that raymond brought from dunham for full articulation of the colored body/ it hurt/ was exhilarating and empowering/raymond callt what we were learning african-american dance/ the same as afro-cuban/haitian/ or afro-brazilian dance/ there was something to us/ we gave two concerts a year/ under the auspices of the afro-american historical society and marcus books/ this is where i met paula moss who helped me develop the "choreopoem"/ and rosalie alphonso, the filipina who was one of the first "colored" girls/ raymond used live drummers/ while stanze peterson did not/ there i met tomasin medal in exile from nicaragua/ this is how my aesthetic was internationalized/ and came to be/ i realized that i wrote differently and more forcefully after class/ that the movements propelled the language and/or the language propelled the dance/ it is possible to start a phrase with a word and end with a gesture/ that's how i've lived my life/ that's how i continue to study/ produce black art.

    i wanted to run away from graduate school/ to dance
    with sun ra/ they said he'd still be there/ wait
    i heard my mother sing along with sun ra's ellington
    i had my daughter blessed by sun ra with his
    golden crown/ her little feet move to max roach on
    7th avenue/ there is magic in those drums/ & in those feet/
    clda asked miles davis what he heard
    my mother heard sterling brown//

movement/ melody/ muscle/
meaning/ mcintyre

CHANTS THAT MUST BE SUNG. MUSIC THAT MUST BE heard, to pacify spirits, consecrate our souls, we sometimes call magic. Dianne McIntyre calls it dance. Her company, Sounds in Motion, is such a force that we must repent, rethink, reinvent, remember all our lives cause it's urgent. And we're strong. No matter how the 20th century has denigrated the human body, the black people, the land, McIntyre's choreography insists that living is arduous and remarkable. Her suites, *Life's Force* (1979) and *Shadows* (1975), push the dancers till we cannot believe they could move again. Another leg cannot extend. Who could leap? Where is breath for a contraction more? How is it possible? And that is McIntyre's point. Human energy is infinite. We can do more. We must. Even her own solo, *Triptych* (1980), in collaboration with Max Roach and Abbey Lincoln, was an unrelenting assault on her body. Her innate lyricism sustaining her, grace under pressure, a city dweller's rosary.

McIntyre's pieces are the legacy of millions of Americans who are here because their forebears did what they had to. Their lives depended on it. That's how McIntyre's Sounds in Motion performs her work: Like if they don't do these dances, they might die. At the Symphony Space, February 7, McIntyre resurrected *Memories* (1975) and *Union* (1974). These are dissimilar pieces requiring different skills and approaches from the dancers, as well as challenging their resourcefulness to make an old dance new. The core of the group, Bernadine Jennings, Lonnetta Gaines, Mickey Davidson, Fred Davis, Ahmed Abdullah, and Babafumi Akunyun, has been with McIntyre since the mid '70s.

I first saw *Memories* in 1974 at the Henry Street Settlement House. Since that time McIntyre's work has become more complex spatially and rhythmically, moving toward sculpted impulse and labyrinthine density. Yet *Memories* highlights certain basic McIntyre aesthetics: reliance on popular Afro-American dance; respect for Afro-American music; and a sense of the conceptual realities available to us through these forms. It is not that McIntyre's work rejects folklore, but her versions of what is folkloric are formed by the here and now. There are no accidental ethnic references. It is all on purpose.

By the time the regal Lonnetta Gaines as The Woman in *Memories* has settled in her chair and quieted, we know that this black woman is a particular history. She conjures visions of special moments she has to remember or acquiesce the numbness. Eubie Blake's early compositions with Noble Sissle propel her visitors, Her Mother and Her Father. Portrayed by Gwendolyn Nelson-Fleming and Fred Davis. Nelson-Fleming's return to

Sounds in Motion after a long absence is gratifying. Her full body and light feet remind us that dance is not restricted to those slight of limb.

The parents' "couple-dancing," in all its sexuality and fun, is how The Woman remembers them. These characters are not Puritan America. They are black America, facile, sensual, and hopeful, as evidenced by McIntyre's solo as With Hopes. Bernadine Jennings' presence, as With Despair, elicits wonder at the length of her legs and the reach of her eyes. Sashaying with her battered broom, Jennings' body rejects pity, succumbs to the fatigue a cleaning woman must know, and startles to an innocent joie de vivre if she steals a moment to dream. Mickey Davidson, With Love, beguiles with the precision of her movements, the tenacity of her body. Coupled with Phillip Bond, Young Man, there are allusions to Ailey's *Fix Me Jesus* duet from *Revelations.*

Memories is a rare McIntyre composition in that it is linear. There is a narrative line drawing separate elements into our view. From this point on, as demonstrated in *Union,* the only lines McIntyre's concerned with are geometric emotional architectures, personal landscapes created with the bodies of her dancers. McIntyre hankers for flat repeating horizontals, punctuated by suspended contracted torsos, rectangular leaps, arched turns, and squared hips. McIntyre shapes territories for her dancers. They are not exiles. They are not without a place where they are in control.

The South African horizons evoked by Ahmed Abdullah's trumpet ease Jennings across the floor. Akunyun's brilliant percussion pushes Bond, Davis, and Brown off the ground explosively. Muneer's cello, positioned like an electric bass, tosses Davidson, Banks, and Gaines off center toward flexed images: craters, torn fences, skyscrapers in a quake. Gwendolyn Nelson-Fleming's voice rides over it all like the wind, a siren, a mother's wail. The musicians of Sounds in Motion give credence to the possibilities of old-fashioned call and response in a modern American dance company.

That McIntyre includes the verse of Langston Hughes and Margaret Walker doesn't mean her dance is not saying something she wanted to say. Rather, McIntyre assumes responsibility for accurate portrayals of our history: letting who said it first take credit, take part in the continuing struggle. This is why there is no end to *Union*. The company is literally flying, cutting the air, as the lights fade. The music goes on. Our lives depend on our coming together. While we breathe, there can be no bows. There is no rest.

The Harlem Cultural Council's persistent efforts to present contemporary choreographers is paying off. Had it not been for the Dancemobile Winter Series, McIntyre might not have ever reconstructed *Memories* or *Union*. We would not have had the opportunity to see her consistently vigorous use of the black female body—Jennings, Gaines, and Davidson belie the notion that strong women are masculine. We are primordial energies: molten, direct, irrepressible. Just watch a Jennings stride. Her extensions could push laser beams out of her way. Davidson's energy rushes through her fingers so that her body is electric.

McIntyre's commitment to improvisation, so that her dancers make their own statements within the rubrics of sound and sweat, is the foundation of a company that does not lie. When Sounds in Motion moves, they mean it. Our lives depend on this.

did i hear the
congregation say amen?

I'll play something and she takes it and runs. She is one of the
great black singers in the tradition of all other great singers . . .
the black woman who's dealing with the new music. She does not
back off.

—Andrew Cyrille

JEANNE LEE DOES NOT NEED A BAND. SHE DOES NOT
need to tell us to come to her. She does not need a microphone or
electricity. There is nothing an elevator could do for Jeanne Lee.
She sings, sometimes with the Galaxy Dream Band and sometimes on her own. But she sings. Did I hear the congregation say
Amen?

At Soundscape a couple of weeks ago, Jeanne Lee performed

The Poem as Song/The Song as Ritual. On 52nd Street I realized Jeanne Lee is clothed and fed by her voice. That's the same street my aunts and uncles were born black on, so 52nd and 10th means something to me—like a people who come out with what they can carry: love, sweat, blood and song. Though everything we know is wonderful and rich, we, as a people, hide, to keep it safe. Jeanne Lee don't. Jeanne Lee didn't hide behind her dancers or her musicians though it would have been easy, with the likes of Andrew Cyrille on drums and percussion, Gunter Hampel on vibes, bass clarinet, flute, and piano, Thomas Keyserling on alto sax and flute, William Parker on bass and Rrata Christine Jones's dance.

Aretha addresses God. Billie Holiday seduced him. Tina Turner made the devil think twice/ but Jeanne Lee is mingling among us.

Just take a stroll down Seventh Avenue
and tip your hat
to everyone you meet
You see the world
on Seventh Avenue;
it's in the eye of everyone you meet.
Just tip your hat,
your heart,
your soul,
your feet
and greet the world
in ev'ry 'I' you meet . . .
Say, "How are you,
and you, and you
and you. How do you do,"
ya do ya do ya

do . . . (improv.)
—Jeanne Lee, Wellspring

She is not afraid of all this body that moves so sweet I dare you/ and isn't this more than you ever imagined; her body is song. Moses as a child would have flown on his bed of rushes had she been singing by the Nile.

> *"why you call the moon*
> *His majesty?"*
> *"well baby,*
> *the moon is like a man, to me;*
> *doin' all his fine*
> *little tricks and show*
> *with the clouds,*
> *and then comes beamin' out*
> *so proud*
> *and sure*
> *of himself.*
> *For me,*
> *the sun is a woman;*
> *round*
> *and warm*
> *and*
> *life giving.*
> *Maybe they're each*
> *a little bit of both."*
> *"Amen.*
> *You got it baby.*
> *mmmmmm—Lawd!*
> *I'm so HAPPY 'bout dis child."*
> —Jeanne Lee, Conversations

It is such a relief to meet a wild black woman and live where she lives among those she has chosen. Now we could visit at home listing and sharing her records. The collaborations with Jimmy Lyons and Andrew Cyrille, Nuba (Black Saint), or the remarkable *Blase* (BYG) with Archie Shepp, but then we could have Ms. Lee all to ourselves on her own record *Conspiracy* (Earthforms). If we still can't get enough, there is always the Lee-Hampel discography to explore. *Journey to the Song Within* (Birth), *Enfant Terrible* (Birth), and *Out from Under* (Birth) have never left me wanting.

Her voice is full like Chaka Khan's, or soft like young Gloria Lynne. There is the ache of an Etta James, sometimes, in the heights of Minnie Riperton before she knew pain. Makeba's insolence as well as the sensual hush of Leci Brandão slip in. From time to time, it's just/ Jeanne Lee.

It is enough to say I heard about Mahalia. My grandma told me 'bout Clara Ward. But I saw Jeanne Lee. Maybe there are too many of us with too much need/ so we *have* to not sing. We have to listen for the Word. Lee leads us up and out of Cyrille's percussive melodies, through the swinging Chicago spaces Rrata C. Jones creates. Well. Did the congregation say Amen?

Jeanne Lee can't talk unless she moves, and one thought would not occur without the other. Here we've got a tradition who could be like Dindga McCannon and Chase-Riboud's sculptures, flowing in space. We got a woman among us who isn't afraid of the sound of her own voice. She might lay up nights, wondering how we are staying alive 'cause we didn't hear what she just heard/ or sing it. Well. Did I hear the congregation say Amen?

She sings.

Jeanne Lee/ She sings.

a celebration of black survival/ black dance america/ brooklyn academy of music/ April 21–24, 1983

Journal Entry #692
what does it mean that blk folks cd sing n dance?
why do we say that so much/ we dont know what we mean/
i saw what that means/ good god/ did i see/ like i cda
walked on the water myself/ i cda clothed the naked & fed
the hungry/ with what dance i saw tonite/ i don't mean dance
i mean a closer walk with thee/ a race thru swamps that fall
off in space/ I mean i saw the black people move the ground
& set stars beneath they feet/ so what's this mean that
black folks cd dance/ well/ how abt a woman like dyane harvey
            who can make
her body the night riders & the runaways/ the children hangin
on they mama's dress/ while they father's beat to death/ the

blood/ from de man's wounds/ his woman's tears/ the night riders
goin off in the darkness/ the silence of the night
how abt bernadine j. whose body waz all of that in 5 min-
utes/ & whose very presence humbled all but the drum/
now that's a dance/ like rael lamb careenin cross
the stage on his bare stomach/ fifty feet/
sounds like possums n rattlesnakes/ mississippi undercurrents
& steamin hog maws/ tossin him from decatur to south texas/
tearin him from contraction to leaps so expansive/ his body
took the space allowed thirty redwood trees/ & those sounds
kept pushin him/ little racing motors like the cops waz
round the bend/ windows opened & shut cuz there are things
others ought not to hear/ feet on stairways of burned out homes/
the sounds pushed him/ & there was a dance that was a black
dance/ that's what it means that black folks cd dance/ it
dont mean we got rhythm/ it dont mean the slop or the hully
    gully/
or this dance in houston callt "the white boy"/ it dont mean just
what we do all the time/ it's how we remember what cannot be
    said/
that's why the white folks say it aint got no form/ what was the
    form
of slavery/ what was the form of jim crow/ & how in the hell
    wd they know . . .
N. Shange, *Sassafrass, Cypress & Indigo*

What do we mean by this racist cliché that all black folks can
sing and dance? Some answers were provided by Dance Black
America, April 21 through 24, 1983, at the Brooklyn Academy
of Music. The Festival afforded us an intellectual as well as aesthetic immersion in the realms of Afro-American movement
since Diaspora, also known as slavery. Colloquia examining re-

gional and folk dance, the legacy and implications of Dunham, and our relationships to Latin and African forms were preparations for performances and choreographic exploration by Afro-Americans from all over the country.

Many of these movers I have seen before.

In the basement of a church in Harlem, Chuck Davis teaches till sweat seeps from the floor and the spirits of the drums push ancient Africa from our modern black bodies. On East 12th Street in New York City, Rod Rodgers is free in movement and committed through dance to the end of racism, nuclear war, and hunger. Uptown at Sounds in Motion on Lenox Avenue, Dianne McIntyre utilizes what we know of Cunningham, Horton, and Graham with the force of her slight body: herself, dance. Downtown Eleo Pomare in his dances addresses muscle and the patient strength that has kept Afro-Americans in the New World from disappearing from the face of the earth. His *Las Desenamoradas* is more than a realization of the pain of being "the unbeloved." It is a singular effort to find the believable in the midst of despair: the impossible.

Chuck Davis's *Lenjen-Go/Mandiani,* Rod Rodgers' *Box,* Dianne McIntyre's *Etude in Free*—only part of this marvelous distillation of our struggle to survive: Dance Black America.

Donny McKayle's *Rainbow* is one gift my mother gave me; his lyricism is still "una regalo," a gift. *Road of the Phoebe Snow,* Talley Beatty's contribution to the program, is one of the more technically difficult pieces of our time. I saw it performed admirably, courageously, by the Alvin Ailey Repertory Ensemble. Blondell Cummings performed her *Chicken Soup,* in which the kitchen is the center of our lives. Once in San Francisco, she and I planted fifty-five bulbs of flowers, to bloom as black dance in America should bloom. We are a blossoming people, "floras negras." Louis Johnson once stopped me on Grove Street to say we must dance. His *Forces of Rhythm,* performed impeccably by the Philadelphia Dance Company, fuses classical, modern, ethnic, and jazz styles, showing us how to dance, and why.

We must sing and dance or we shall die an inert, motionless, "sin ritmo" death. "Negros muertos," killed by a culture afraid of who we are and what we have to say with our bodies, our music, and our brains. Black folks do have brains. We even have ideologists, scholars, choreographers, and always the grace of the gods . . . although my teacher, Fred Benjamin, sometimes tests Christ, inviting Mary Magdalene to pick up her skirts and switch a bit to the beat of her soul: our souls—a collective whole. One people, one motion in myriad forms. Ask VèVè Clark, the dance scholar, what she does in Haiti. I assure you, bad back or not, she's not reading books. She's dancing. Between the legendary feet of Pepsi Bethel and the jazz of us all, between Charles Moore and "el afro-latino de nosotros," there is a space open to all human beings unafraid of the ferocity of a people who take dance seriously, who seriously dance, and are generous enough to share.

Such as *Lenjen-Go/Mandiani,* performed by the Chuck Davis Dance Company:

Listen to the drum from Congo Square to East 110. Lift those feet! Swing those arms! Become a swan who sees something she can't resist up in the sky somewhere. Chuck Davis demonstrates it, brightly.

Lots of critics only talk about our costumes, our colors. That's true, we are a people of color, with color. We cula ful: yellow, violet, green, orange, pink, and always black. Many rows of women, hips back and forth, east to west; young men in the throes of the drum as we all are, if we feel it. Never forgetting the flexibility of our backs—today our necks, in different circumstances. We sing. We dance. As VèVè Clark said at one of the festival's symposia, the question is not "What is black dance," but "What it is." Dance on. Pat those feet through the soil. Let those toes grip the earth we worked. We don't need no shoes. We need to dig and jump into the land we come from; one woman after another, one dream upon the other, calling up who we are. If there are still questions about the angers of Afro-American dance, look only at the bent knees, fluid backs, vigorous arms of the Chuck Davis Dance Company. "No hay nada mas de discutar." Such as Arthur Hall's *Marie Laveaux and Danse Congo Square,* performed by the Arthur Hall Afro-American Dance Ensemble:

Through a remarkable golden raffia emerge dancers as slaves, looking for a moment to, as Larry Graham says, "puleese release yourself." In this piece the European influence of the New World is already apparent in the "danzon" nature of the movement and the coupling off of male and female. At that time we were merely property with rhythm. In Curaçao, Martinique, Vera Cruz, and Charleston we danced these dances, a strange syncretism of "las Siete Potencias," the Seven Powers, and for what we had become in the New World, manifest in the walk of Arthur Hall.

The excerpt from Hall's *Fat Tuesday,* a high ceremony of candles, sequins, and drums, with a deity draped in yellow and black, undulating under marvels of feathers, takes us back once again to some form of parity. A movement not defiled, or at least not violated, though we all know the truth of the matter. In West Africa, Elegua is an old and crippled man. Think for a moment: our crossroad was an ocean. Double-dutch to sand-dancing, roller discos to Lucume, alive and well in Cuba. There is always a continuity to our movement, subtle, erotic, informed by history, known and unknown.

"Hambone, Hambone, have you hear." Seven young men stomp out, letting us know that the gracious beauty of the disco dances emerges from the crudity and unselfconsciousness of our workers—our ancestors, called slaves. We make minstrelsy our own, even wearing red velvet, but no burnt cork. Our dance reflects the many ways we've avoided death, insisted on living. For the beat, for the heat, for the freedom of dance. Ain't no way to keep us down on no ground; we just jump up again and again and again.

A brass band and saxophones leading us to someone's promised land. An old New Orleans procession, right here in Brooklyn. Like we don't have to go so far to get home. Dejan's Olympia Brass Band of New Orleans can always see me "home" by the mercy of our Lord Jesus Christ, whose cross appears in the sky as the band escorts the lost soul to the Promised Land. Very bright colors, of course, because nothing stops Carnival.

Such as Lenwood Sloan's *Darktown Strutters' Ball/ Strut Miss Lizzie,* danced by Halifu Osumare and Leon Jackson, with Neal Tate on the piano and Ruth Brisbane singing:

So black et rouge. We've been everywhere; ask Josephine or Katherine. Our music and dance is our answer to our interaction with the world—all of it, from Clark Air Force Base in Manila to Guantánamo. A black somebody felt something enough to move him/her: "Let's do it, let's do it till we can't stand no mo'."

In Oakland, California, at Everybody's Creative Arts Center Halifu Osumare breathes, relaxes. Her movement reflects today and yesterday. Tonight at BAM, in *All the Dusky Gals Were There,* Osumare is enchanting as any Southern belle could be, including Scarlett O'Hara. She and her partner, Leon Jackson, exhibit the delicacy we have managed to sustain throughout the bombing of Tulsa, the riots of Liberty City, and "white only" water fountains. We have a grace about us that Dunham may have called the ability to stretch. We are all ready at the barre. The stretch is survival.

Such as the Navy Yard Boys Club Sea Cadets' *Pickin' Em Up and Puttin' Em Down:*

Military grouping. "Cultura y Armas." In case you forgot there's a struggle going on here. In Nicaragua, El Salvador, St. Alban's, Angola—seems like everywhere black folks live, we gotta be ready to fight. Turn about and open ranks in your sunglasses and apple jack caps. Defend our right to make art. 1-2-3-4. Turn to the rear. Cover your back. You are too precious to lose, to abandon here in Brooklyn. Dance on, guns in hand. Who would know which was make-believe, the guns or our spirit? Who would dare take a chance on making a mistake?

Such as *Harlem Rent Party,* an assembly of dances performed by Mama Lu Parks' Jazz Dancers:

Take some tap dancing, a boa or two, and black hips: "now that gonna be a dance." Our bodies become our instruments. No trumpets, but some feet that don't miss a beat, and never missed the "A Train." Shakin', shakin' up past 59 Street, straight to 125, where we all know what the step is. Especially for a rent party, where we doin *Sweet Georgia Brown.* Pick up them feet. Pass the hat. Oh, remember the Apollo amateur nights. Now Mama Lu Parks with a young Sammy Davis tap-dancing with a younger Debbie Allen. Time step, triple that, and break-it-on-down. Where'd you put that accent, boy? This is the real deal. Don't mess around 'less you really planning on 'messin' with it.

In Brazil, we play the dozens with "Capoeira." Here in America, English-speaking, we play the dozens with taps and our tongues. But there's always a winner—an older man, experienced warrior of rhythm like Al Perryman. For without our drums, there's only our hands and feet, the voice of a people supposedly inarticulate, assumed inaudible. But James Brown and Little Anthony never had problems being heard, nor did George Jackson.

Silently, moving along like Sojourner in the night, moving on toward liberty.

But right now, we gonna Lindy Hop. Pachucos and black folks loving for the moment of glory, when we move. War or no war, what has our life been: one long marathon dance. Pass that hat. The rent's due. Dance it up. Dance it away. Ballet shoes aren't enough to say alla this. Get those feet up off the ground and put them women up in the air. This here's a life dance. It's hard, and full of travail. Get them feet off of the ground. Reach for the world. Take it.

"You Could Have Been Anything You Wanted To," the Biss Harmonizers sing for us, bringing us to our childhoods and recent history of corner du-wop. "Babee, how could I let you get away?" Where did we let black dancers go? Can we find a place in our hearts for all we been missing? Can we get a hold to it now? Who is looking for Sonora Matancera or Celia Cruz? Who is looking for Pepsi Bethel of Sounds in Motion? Elijah said we were the lost-found people. Let's find ourselves now. It's in the beat, the beat called destiny.

We could paint our way out like Doze, spray can in hand behind the Jazzy Double Dutch Jumpers, but foreigners call that graffiti. Fab 5 Freddy says we can rap our way out, but the foreigners call that illiterate. What is the path to freedom, and how many ways can we get there? Dance on. Rap on. "Don't Stop 'Til You Get Enough." Smurf on, brothers. Just don't hurt yourself, man. Be a little more gentle on them black bones. Listen to Master Blaster. He say, "It's called survival. Only the strong can survive." And it's true, black folks do sing, and glory hallelujah, we do dance, dance we do.

bang on!

LAST SUMMER I HAD THE PRIVILEGE TO ONCE AGAIN experience Billy Bang in person. Buoyant, gritty, and melodic at once, his playing evoked *Bama Swing* whether the tune was "bama" or not. There is in the quality of Billy's playing a sense of studied urgency, humor, and reverence for the fragility and resilience of the wood and string, horsehair and craftsmanship that makes a violin one that will come alive. Although I doubt that Bang would find any violin dead weight, the energy he is able to generate in this instrument that has struggled so hard for its voice in the jazz arena is startling, unnerving and reassuring simultaneously.

I first encountered Billy Bang on my late-night sojourns to

hear charanga and pachanga bands where the violin is a percussive instrument, not to the supper clubs like the Rainbow Room where the violin sings, threatening no one. That cannot be said of Bang's bowing or chordal flights towards the talking drum. Even *Sweet Georgia Brown* which I had found perfected by Stuff Smith comes alive again with Bang's specific articulation leading directly to comparisons with the horns (Philip Harper, or Lee Morgan), woodwinds (Albert Ayler, Arthur Blythe, Hamiet Bluiett), and the quick brilliant feet of tap dancers (Savion Glover, Mickey Davidson), sand dancers (Norma Miller), and Lena Horne in the window before she turns to sing. This anticipation, not knowing how a phrase we think we know is going to present itself, is particularly true in the Bang composition *Peaceful Dreams,* where not unlike Sun Ra, with whom *Bang played* intermittently over the years, solace can be found in risk. The lyrical qualities Bang is able to draw from this instrument while persisting in rigorous bowing innovations allow the sounds to hover in the air, over our bodies, not unlike Cecil Taylor's quieter moments and Muhal Richard Abrams' raucous seductions of the piano. From the violin with Bang fly references to everything we know about black music and a lot we've yet to learn about rhythm, subtlety, and swing. Bang's technical facility in the upper registers of the violin, in positions past third where the neck of the violin is cradled in his hand while his fingers reach eagerly toward the bridge, is evident in his composition *Spirits Entering.*

On *Three Faces of Eve* Bang almost seems to challenge Latin jazz virtuoso Alfredo de la Fé, whose skillful fingering and brilliant bowing can make us believe violins spit bullets that not only hum, but shout and take solos before hitting their marks. This softly salsa-inspired piece permits Billy Bang to take on arpeggios as assaults without losing a keen hold on the beauty of speed in harmony with pianist D. D. Jackson, drummer Ronnie Burrage, and bassist Akira Ando. Bang's pizzicato on *Yesterdays* is just a touch of the miracles he is capable of with his left hand, fingers taunting the speed of sound if not of light. While in *Don's Dream* Bang falls back on the keys and weight of southern work songs before venturing into a melodic riff that will befuddle those who think Bang loses control of the bow when playing passionately.

To those I say, Billy Bang can play circles around whatever he last did, while jumping up and down on one foot which he sometimes does with his spats, silk forties suits, and bowler hats. I've even seen Billy Bang mistake himself for a Senegalese acrobat, violin in hand, and never miss a note, a beat, an insinuation of what's possible which is so amazing about the violin. We don't know what all is possible. But, I can assure you, even if he's at reunion of the Heliocentric Arkestra, Peter Pan hat, Robin Hood cape, and all, Billy Bang cannot be dismissed. The violin with all its medieval trappings comes knock, knock, knockin' on our imaginations and the legacy of our people doesn't even ask who's there. It's just Bang. Billy, that is.

2 live crew

IN HER NEW COLLECTION OF POETRY, *THE VENUS Hottentot* (University of Virginia, 1990), Elizabeth Alexander documents and explores the historical relationship between sexuality, humiliation, 'otherness,' and dignity in patriarchal Western society, drawing directly from the experience of a Xhosa woman from Cape Town, who in the 1820s was on display in a circus 'curated' by an entrepreneurial scientist, Monsieur Cuvier. Eventually, "Her genitalia/ will float inside a labled/ pickling jar in the Musée/ de l'Homme." In her fabulated voice Alexander pronounces the Venus' interior worlds:

Monsieur Cuvier investigates
between my legs, poking, prodding,

sure of his hypothesis.
I half expect him to pull silk
scarves from inside me, paper poppies,
then a rabbit! He complains
at my scent and does not think
I comprehend . . .

But there are hours in every day
to conjure my imaginary
daughters, in banana skirts

and ostrich-feather fans.
Since my own genitals are public
I have made other parts private.

We viscerally recognize the exploitation here; the wrenching terror of a 'natural woman' demeaned publicly beyond rational interpretation. This was over one hundred and fifty years ago when most of us in the New World were in collective bondage, when the rape and molestation of American women was simply one more oppressive instrument of slavery. The black woman as a freak, geek, soulless, sensual vessel of perverse capacities, not at all unlike a dog in heat. That was in slavery times. Those were the perceptions and bestial acts of slavers and European cultural chauvinism gone hog wild. We know this. We denounce this. Shake our heads, relieved that this is no longer true. Look again. Listen again, if you imagine that we as AFRICAN WOMEN have shaken off the violence of slavery which was as nasty as anyone of us could fathom. Gang rapes. Forced rapes. Sex without consent (which is rape). Oral sex as a spectator sport. Love among the black people, a fun-house of mirrors.

This is the world view and supposedly politically correct

stance of Miami rappers 2 Live Crew, whose members were ar-
rested in Florida, for violation of local obscenity laws. In his
own words, Luther Campbell, leader of the group and head of
Skyywalker Records, told CBS's *48 Hours,* "I like bitches. Don't
you like bitches?" Later on another African American man asked
the journalist, "Isn't this America? What about free speech? What
about my rights?" On the Geraldo Show, Campbell added that
the Florida attorney general was really indicting his group because they were black men speaking in their own words.

There is, in fact, a terrible legacy of legal and extra-legal hos-
tility toward the African American male's pronouncement of
his intellectuality and even more, a desperate vengeance toward
an African American man who dared explore his own human-
ity. Yet in LL Cool J to Big Daddy Kane and 2 Live Crew we
find an intent on "stamping out" the brains, hearts, and soul of
the African American woman and all our daughters. It is also,
sadly enough, true that the intellects of African American
males from Ishmael Reed and Harry Allen to Arsenio Hall are
methodically involved in legitimizing the aesthetic of a sound
whose intrinsic, lyric, and dangerously misogynist tendencies
are some sort of culture. The literary progeny of Alexander
Crummell have spent what must be millions of hours conduct-
ing public forums attacking black women writers like Alice
Walker, Toni Morrison, Gayl Jones, and myself for depictions
of African American men that they view as negative. Yet in
their own works, such as *Loup Garou* from Ishmael Reed, the
heroic and deft cowboy-sleuth-hoodoo-man never comes to
the aid of African American women, in fact or fiction.

Nevertheless, for a number of years the clarion cry from the
wings of black male literati is that they have been wronged;
they don't abuse us, molest us, torture us with verbal and physical humiliations. Yet it is commonly known that one out of

three American women will be raped or molested in her life-time. The "smart set" of the black male brotherhood like their rapping compatriots, apparently, exclude us, the black women, from generic American-ness and, specially, womanhood as human. After all, Luther Campbell likes bitches.

In "The Offering" Gus Savage admonishes his 'boys' to "go on ahead and beat u a black woman, but don't hit white women cause they don't like it."

This is America, right? This is the land of our fathers (not incest specific here), where the likes of Celie, Cypress, Sula, Peola, Corregidora, and Tookie and Queen Latifah try valiantly to claim some small integrity for themselves in fiction. In real life, like the Hottentot Venus, we make other parts private, since our genitals are exposed: Nasty as They Wanna Be and Poison and N.W.A. (Niggaz With Attitude) doesn't just fuck the police. The current masculine ethos eschews the beauty and romance implicit in the melodies of the Flamingos, Nat King Cole, Otis Clay, Son Seals, Jackie Wilson, and Smokey Robinson with For Men Only rejoinders to relish our degradation, sloppy seconds & all: crooning that insane idea that they have that "no" means "yes." It is sad that these new African American male anthems allow the fellas themselves no intimate sensuality, no vulnerability, and apparently there is no sense that sexual prowess is thoughtful as opposed to brutal. There's no mention of condoms or pregnancy, gonorrhea or chlamydia. Nowhere do these popular locker-room chants acknowledge AIDS. Everywhere, the all-male chorus shouts gleefully," if you don't comply, "We'll make you." This kind of talk is dangerous to the lives of women and girls.

Our daily interaction with men in our community is compromised when the integrity of our bodies and persons is assaulted by the violent refrains of the likes of 2 Live Crew and the Ghetto Boys. These little ditties do not simply portray African American women negatively. These contrite couplets by our brothers create a climate where rape is the conclusion of any relationship with a black woman. Hey, rape is a crime: a felony. This is not about images. This is about the safety of women and girls in the company of African American men who walk around chanting rhymes about doing harm at random to any one of us. If there's more of them than there are of us, so what? Talk about a derailed Soul-Train! The guys on the Arsenio Hall Show pose as family figures who really don't let their daughters listen to this sort of thing. Is that the point? I'm concerned about what their sons have got pumping through their minds, since that's where their dicks are. Did the likes of Prince, Milli Vanilli, and M.C. Hammer, who seem to enjoy their own sexuality enough make the rappers in sweats nervous about theirs?

It is very important, Luther Campbell reminds us, that "I'm using the language of the community. This is how we talk to [one another]." At least M.C. Hammer smiles and is delighted with his own seduction of himself as well as the stairway of undulating young women who also get to say that seething double-entendre: "Ya can't touch this." This is amazing since our literary patriarchy—Mel Watkins, Reed, Allen, Caldwell, to the rest of the pack throw in a couple of nationalists—are rushing to get in line behind the hip hop gangs, slap five, say a few muthafucks, look over their shoulders to see who else is comin (no pun intended), and drop they pants too! Remember, "our genitalia are exposed." The silence of the black male intellectuals regarding the First Amendment compromises implicated by the arrest of 2 Live Crew, misogynist performers, and record dealers selling *Nasty as They Wanna Be* is about as nasty as you can get while the slightest revocation of an African American man's articulation of his reality is an injustice we cannot allow. This peculiar quiet must be rooted in their agreement with 2 Live Crew. How cowardly not to admit their fraternity with blatant woman-haters. Hey, the black bookworms are having new experiences now, being considered among and one of the "brothahs." Tell me, does it feel good, guys? I keep hearing Hammer's voice in *U Can't Touch This* careening down hallways and off corners in the high squeals and raw screams of women and girls muffled and struggling: Ya cain't touch me, can't touch this. Don't touch me. That's the signified response to the call of 2 Live Crew. Again "Our Genitalia are exposed" I haveta holler clear like Hammer: "Don't make me hurt you."

Tell me, how does it feel, fellas, now that you're one of the pack?

iii.

the couch

LONG BEFORE I'D COME TO KNOW MYSELF AS "NTOZAKE"
or a writer, I had wanted to be a psychiatrist. This no doubt had
something to do with my parents' involvement with hospitals,
sick people, poor black people, and me following along to wards,
living rooms, boarding houses, examination rooms, and dark
rooms where X-rays were read or where violently mentally dis-
turbed folks were sequestered. As a surgeon, my father excised
with delicacy what was malignant, diseased, out of tune with the
body; while my mother, as I understood it, assisted individuals or
families to get in tune with society as a whole, to make "living"
work for them as opposed to against them, without necessarily
challenging anything about the world as we know it. Both these
approaches left me wanting. What if what was wrong couldn't

be seen or couldn't be excised? What if life as some soul knew it wasn't worth living without some violent catharsis? I credited Toussaint L'Ouverture and Dessalines, Tubman and Anthony with whatever legitimacy I had, and they were not the sort who 'fit' in. I'd seen *Snake Pit* in all its simplified black-and-white depiction of living in our world with a pained contorted mind and spirit. I was caught somewhere in between the institution of slavery and the lost cells of the Bastille. Surely there is somewhere more peaceful than the ER or the Settlement House. My ultimate answer was the analyst's couch, but before that I had to learn to live with myself madly for a while longer.

I saw things. I was not delusional or schizophrenic, I apparently could reach areas of my unconscious as a child that never left me, which turned out to be as much a burden as a blessing. I had visions. I wasn't playing. I was laying on the grass or upside a great tree, listening and seeing historical figures, artists, people I didn't know dancing with me, taking me to salons in Paris or a roadhouse in Alabama. I was daydreaming, I imagine, but I never diminished those episodes to anything less than my "real life." That's why journalists have such a hard time fact-checking stories on or about me. I will give them an anecdote which is impossible to chart in any methodology. They ask me did something happen and I'll probably say yes, because I remember my dreams, both night and day, as authentically as I experience my daily life. Before I started menstruating, this issue of truth was very much alive. What I believed or felt I could not prove to anybody in a reasoned fashion. That's why I knew instinctively that I should not argue or debate at a certain point, I knew my "truth" was simply mine and not collectively recognized reality. Yet it could not be a lie because I thought/felt it. The only place I know where anybody else believes this is the psychoanalyst's office. There it is enough, to paraphrase Marie Cardinal, to find "the words to say it."

That's why I dance. I can't always find the "words" to say it. I've come to believe there are words as we know them for some things; that the body has a grammar for these constructs which are not beyond articulation, but of another terrain. I'm becoming trans-lingual so that I may speak myself. Maybe I was a passionate gopi girl at Krishna's feet, I don't know. I do know that my body extorts from me what hangs silent in the air. That's why psychopharmacology can only take me so far. I need my body to talk to me. My analyst watches all these gestures of mind and body, listens as closely to my muscle burns or prone attitude turns as my dreams.

Most of my characters have visions and dreams with which some of you are acquainted. Bessie Smith and Billie Holiday visit Sassafrass. Indigo speaks with the sprits of the moon and the ancestors. Everybody, even The Magician, in *Spell #7* opens their interior world to the whole of the audience, though no one else in the scene itself is aware of Allegra brushing her hair or Maxine collecting gold chains that bound her in resistance of the Middle Passage. Liliane actually has an analyst. No. he's not my analyst, he is Lili's. Sean, the debonair photographer in *A Photograph: Lovers in Motion*, needed an analyst. I didn't give him one. I let him suffer. He didn't have any visions, couldn't talk to spirits, shoot the breeze with his own myths, memory weighed too heavily. An example is simply that "my father hadda monkey/ he like better than me," from the mouth of a grown man who is still that little boy. Did that "happen" to me? Not in the material world. But, living with my being, I know that if I "know" about it, it happened to me, belongs to me now. I was not here during the French Revolution, but I can describe Marat's bath and exude

Charlotte Corday's rage and naivete. Just as I named Crack Annie's daughter Beneatha in honor of Hansberry's Beneatha. There is no doubt in my mind that Walter Lee woulda smoked everything in that house away and pledged the money to Beneatha's African boyfriend to get himself in on some wild Dallas-Chicago-Lagos drug deal. Was I conscious of this? No. Can I discuss all this eccentric personal peculiarity now? Yes. Without heart palpitations? Yes. Without clammy palms? Yes. Without blinking an eye? No. All of this is very precious. I must keep an eye on my self/s. I've learned this in a yearly, hour by hour, disciplined manner. It was not easy. I was not happy. I was not always careful. It costs a lot. What do I get in the end? Do I get better? How will I know when I get there? I could get coy. Answer, Beckett knew what detained Godot, but we don't know that. I know I don't know that. Anyway, I have a hard time explicating "le texte." The characters never die. The stories never end for me. That's why like Rapunzel I go unravel my loose ends with my psychoanalyst. Nothing is wrong. No one else knows. A pin could drop, but usually what's falling away is not so piercing, not so singular, only the shreds of living I must make space for somewhere in myself/s who is not only the writer and therefore cannot continue to find herself whole solely on blank pages.

One of Simón Bolívar's houses was hexagonal, seated on a cliff in such a way that from any point, he could feel/see land and peoples who could be free. When I lie nestled on the couch in the room of no color and all colors, I am in that house. I am on that cliff. I am one of those people.

the dark room

WHEN *FOR COLORED GIRLS* . . . WAS AT THE HEIGHT OF
its controversy/popularity, I found myself wearing very dark
glasses and large hats so that folks wouldn't recognize me. I
couldn't ride elevators up or down. If someone figured out who
I was, I calmly stated that I was frequently mistaken for "her."
I'd had other occasions in my life, when I was the only African
American in a class or banished to the countryside that my family loved so much, when I'd been known to disassociate, to refer to myself in the third person. Then, I was "Paulette." Now,
Ntozake was repeating the pattern of the girl I'd gleefully left
behind. This was very troubling. I'd just become who I was and
always was in the frenzied act of "disappearing" me. Now, I
confess to discovering many, many roads to oblivion, but rarely

recounted these episodes with warmth or a sense of well-being. So, I did what I thought troubled writers did, I went to my producer, Joseph Papp, to seek counsel. To my alarm, Joe recommended against analysis or other therapies "because, then, my writers can't write anymore." Well, writing I was, living I was not, even though I wasn't always a supporter of my own perceptions. The ability to write in isolation for hours about anything and enjoy it is a gift, but it is not a life. Even I knew this. I could not hide in a dance studio either. My presence was unavoidable, yet unbearable.

Off to find a shrink I went. I was looking for a wizard, some magic, some chant, or breath that might make being me something to look forward to in the morning. I have the capacity to sleep for four days at a time, if I am so inclined. At one point I refused to get up and live my life among the living because my dream life was so much more interesting. Wizards I did not find. I did find that the right shrink/analyst is as important a decision as finding a soul-mate. Anyway, to make a long story less long, I've been involved with over seven mental health care workers in the last twenty years. The overwhelming periods of time spent with three: one psychiatrist, and two analysts. I lost one analyst to the Emergency Room, which he saw as a challenge. Four years of quasi-sane mourning passed before I was able to seek out another with whom I have been working for nearly a decade.

With his help and astounding patience, I have lost my title as "the angriest patient ever encountered during all my years of practice" to become the 1991–93 "Heavyweight Poetry Champion of the World," as you see, a much healthier management of violent proclivities. In all seriousness I've learned to feel what I see. What I've been blessed to conjure in words is no longer two steps removed; my body is not hindrance to my spirit, but a manifestation of it. I am still crazy, but not so afraid with that part of me. I can even tell jokes to my "crazy" person and realize that to be one of my saner moments.

I've dressed up as a "guinea girl," the ones who stole all the basketball players at my school, just to prove that I could be one. That was a session to remember. I've felt I swear the electricity in my body. I've known the ocean and intense heat. All this actually while on the couch. Talk about terrified. Try being the Atlantic Ocean all by yourself in an eight-by-twelve room with ancient fertility statues placed around like buoys on what I guess I took to be signs of land ahead. I don't know that part of myself to this day. I've talked in tongues. I've only been able to do some sessions in Spanish, or a mixture of French and Portuguese. I don't know why. I know that this is all that would come out. Sometimes, I sleep. Other times, Paulette speaks. Her voice is different than mine as Zaki. Sometimes, I want to knock her out, but since we can only use language as a tool or weapon or doll or whatever I need, I learned at least to talk to her, if I am not wildly gesticulating in some recollection of a dream; legs flying, arms of a flamenco dancer, long Balanchine neck I could never actualize outside my "dark room" where things, me, memories, float out of syllable and become benign or empowering, as they must because they are never without meaning.

Joe, my "Art-Daddy" as I called him, was wrong about one thing, not many, but one. Psychoanalysis made me a finer writer, a fuller person and a funnier one, to be sure. I've found characters I would literally shun to be beauteous. I've been able to take on the persona of someone puzzling to me with no need, not a desperate one, to figure her out. I am plumbing the primordial depths of me, not without trepidation, but with a magic I thought I could pick up somewhere in the night. My analyst's Anthony Molino. He's a pet. He lives in Italy and, like a guardian spirit, with me.

dear daddy, "el amor
que tu me das . . ."

I GUESS I'M STILL UP BY SHEER FORCE OF HABIT.
Remember how you'd come in from the hospital after ordinary
people were long in bed? I can still smell the steak sandwiches
from Brunswick St. & the fried shrimp you'd pick up at Five
Points. Just when all the night people/ gamblers pimps whores
B&E men 3rd shifters/ were satisfying their own wants. The car
made a whirring noise that would annoy somebody else. Yet,
even in the country, especially in the country in the vacant night
absent of music and gleeful conversation that old Cadillac
sounded like sweet Miles, solo, muted sweet, a classic. Why today we misst Muhal Richard Abrams and the AACM at that
place that caught fire during a reading of mine!

I guess you should know I never refer to you in the past, even though I know you died. But you know, you died in the middle of the night, your special time & mine. You were driving lonely Jersey highways on the way from a wrestling match. I loved those roads with you, listening to Louis Armstrong or Tito Puente; the distances were always too short. The car, asphalt sliding under our laughter & tales of meeting Dizzy Gillespie or Horace Silver. I met Horace Silver & got Son Seals' autograph on my arm. So I brought something to the table, too. But you knew that.

Daddy, I hope I didn't embarrass you too much when I had you pick me up at Black Jack's in South Trenton, so I could show you my photograph above the bar just when Tookie started to tell you her life story since you brought her into the world & Black Jack came out of his private quarters since it was yr 1st time in his place even though he's been yr patient for years. But, Papa, I knew I cd go to Black Jack's any time I had to dance. Dance hard & fast. Dance how you danced with Mommy with abandon and grace.

You know what else? I don't like the way our family sees yr grave site either. Not that it's not proper. I mean there's an impressive tombstone & some kinda heavy potted perennial. But, Daddy, there should be an earlier installation, by David Hammonds and a Howardena Pindell tapestry should be floating over you to keep evil spirits away & let you feel the evening breeze as she comes to you. Damn, Daddy, I should have gotten Martin Puryear to craft you some sacred cypress wishing web so I cd come in & out of the realms of this world you cherished at will. Then Irma & I, that's Miguel's sister who always thought you were handsome, would get Ricardo the Dominican Santero to come "clean" the whole space. Irma, Miguel, Ricardo & I swam clandestine in the Raritan River & Ricardo washed our heads with fresh coconut milk, right from the shell. That'll do you up just fine & protect you if you go haunting the lil joints in upper Harlem; on the Lower East Side where I paid my dues.

I really appreciated yr not laughing out loud when Felix de Rooy showed that achingly long 35 minutes of film as the Caribbean Christ. He's in Amsterdam now, and you were the only poet's daddy who was present, & fit right in & Adál's still photographing himself.

I wished you stayed here (not that I think you're gone) but I wished you had seen my piece with Ladysmith Black Mambazo, such singing, Daddy. An I've made a personal friend of Archie Shepp, the avant-garde sax man you liked. I know you lifted that left eyebrow and looked somewhere else if I played Cecil Taylor or if Cecil started talking metaphysics. Daddy, I danced in the Tropicana in La Habana like you an Mommy before Fidel. The magic is still there but not the terror. I walked the streets of Johannesburg without a pause, swam in the waters outside Durban, jumping waves in a free South Africa, but my last weeks in Managua were also the end of Sandinista dreams. You wda been so proud of me, riding with Comandante Tomás through the mountains, realizing why the power of the automatic machine gun at my side was not yr weapon of choice. You are too gentle for some of what I know.

Oh, Papa, I can't forget the night you & Mommy stayed up all night in my very bare apt in Dorchester listening to me and Pedro Pietri, all in black with his portable coffins, reading poetry. Pedro came to your church service in the church where they funeralized you. Papa, I came to love your friends too just because they were your friends & knew you in a way I didn't and can't. Wittico, the elegant; Moose, the passionate; J. Minor, the Cherokee chief; and Pops, your soul mate; and Tom Jones, the dreamer, are precious to me. Even though I rarely see them I don't see them any less than you did.

Daddy, I finally got into that beaded strapless outfit you gave me & I didn't stop lifting weights to do it, either. Somehow I grew into it. I wore it the night the National Black Theatre Festival honored me with Ntozake Shange Day. That was in Winston-Salem, North Carolina last summer. Plus, I went to cocktails at Maya Angelou's and spent time with William Marshall and Billy Dee Williams. I wish you had been with us long enough to hear La India, she is an angelic Tina Turner.

Oh, Daddy, on the more somber side, since you've been gone from this plane, whenever I stay up late, like we used to, old black-&-white movies starring Ronald Reagan come on. He has Alzheimer's now, so he can't feel guilt or remorse for the plight of sick people anymore. If he had his whole brain he still wasn't capable of experiencing compassion. Daddy, the era of politics Reagan ushered in has outlived you and more poor & black people are dying, suffering, homeless, violent, desperate for a vision of a world for us like you had.

Daddy, do you think I could help with that? It was only a rumor that CLR was like a father to me. I know I'm not a boy, but forgive the language, Papa. I'm one fierce muther. You did name me after you. You know what else, Daddy? David Murray, my ex-husband, my friends Chico Freeman, Fred Hopkins, Jean-Paul Bourelly, Billy Bang, even Spaceman—every one of them could play a melody that wd make you start swaying yr head so you cd catch every note. You were just as much a part of our posse as Max, Milt, Dizzy, Chico H., and both Andy and Jerry Gonzalez. There's no music I hear without sensing you.

Did I ever really thank you & Mom for bringing gallons of fried chicken, greens and fixins to us when we were sitting in at Hamilton Hall in 1968? Some people's parents stopped speaking to them and cut off tuition. But you fed us. Thank you, Daddy. I know you abhor legions of cops & militant social coups, but we were hungry.

Getting back to yr alleged grave site. Mi novio, Elmo, who's a black Puerto Rican bluesman from Chicago (I thought you'd like that!), anyway he's promised to help me lay handmade glazed bricks in the typical Zócalo formation to let everyone know wherever you are is hallowed ground. That you are yr own tradition & yr space is a place for spirits & people to gather when they're in need of solace. Though Victor Cruz & Alejandro cda blessed the place with poems in tongues & some leftover pine spring water we found by the Russian River years ago, the sacred never runs out, Daddy, only the profane is short-lived.

ellie, who is my mother

"In the fullness of time, we shall know why we are tried and why our love brings us tears as well as happiness."

—the Torah
(my mother's favorite quotation from childhood)

THERE IS A MEMORY OF THE SWISH-SWISHING OF SKIRTS, the smells of powders and coffee, my father's cologne seems to seep from her skin and the pillow where I nestle my head. My whole body curved again as in the beginning. I am the only one. This is my mother, Eloise, who married Paul who was my father and that's how she became my mother.

Mirrors. Small delicate bottles. Dresses with pearls and lace from Paris. I knew this. I saw it on the globe that lit up at night like the neon signs across the way, letting me know we were colored in the colored part of town. Yet the movies and photographs were black-and-white. Not fitting all the different shapes and odors of folks who came to see my mother. Laughter from the kitchen. Laughter up the stairs. Aunt Emma was here, Uncle Jimmy was here with Aunt Margaret. So were my grandmothers. My mother had a special greeting for each one, as if there were something special in her soul that let her know what touch or hug a body needed. My grandmother hovered like Billie Burke. I couldn't distinguish my mother from Jean Seberg, Marilyn Monroe, Kim Novak, or Dorothy Dandridge. I remember her eyes glowed as mine widened when Carmen de Lavallade danced.

The Lindy Hop was not the only vernacular activity my mother mastered. There were collard greens and smothered pork chops. There were nights when sleep came dragging its heels and my mother had a rhythmic pat that was so soft yet steady that sleep gave up staying away from me. Let my mother calm my soul so that when my dreams came, I dreamt in color.

I liked to hide in the back of my mother's closet with her dresses and smells. Now I realize many, many other little girls did the same. Even my own daughter waltzed about in my robe, wrapping my scent about her like some kind of magic.

Once we all wore the same color blue dresses, my sisters, my mother, and I. We were one for a long time. I could not tell long after I should have known better that I was not my mother. I wanted to be my mother. I liked her. I liked the way people liked her. I liked my father. But I could not be him. I could be her. I could deep-sea fish, play baccarat, sing like Marian Anderson, defend the race. We were a vulnerable people. I could tell from the stories my mother told with her friends when they played inscrutable games of cards for hours. Bridge. What did I know then about my mother, this bridge called my back. What do I know now about my mother?

I live with the myth of her, my indisputable legend of her. Executing intricate steps of the cha-cha-cha in La Habana, dressing us all for the March on Washington, surviving disastrous lover after lover that I chose for myself, since I was not my mother. Since I was not my mother, I am still learning to mother myself, which Alta and Adrienne told me years ago. But I couldn't give up the black-and white films of Ellie, who is my mother, to another time or other places. I see horizons sometimes and think of what she saw for me. I am guilty of spending days under huge oaks imagining myself as my mother when I became a mother, yet I am not. I really know I am not my mother, but if I were to ever lose my myth of this woman of independent thought and chutzpah during the fifties, who actually demonstrated the meaning of "each one teach one," I would be less a woman than I am, less a mother than I am becoming. I respect Ellie. Then, sometimes I feel sadly for her because as colorful and colored as we were, our world was defined in black and white. Our world was featured in *Ebony, Jet, Sepia*. Now when I look at us, Ellie and then me and my daughter, something is awry, I become uncollected. I never saw my mother "uncollected." She was not one to accept or expect to survive on Blanche's risky kindness of strangers, nor was she "invisible." But, I'm saving all my images, all the touch recollections I can sustain because the depth of Ellie's presence in me is antediluvian, fierce, and infinite. So unlike what she appears to be, all of which she gave me.

on silk

I COULD SAY, IMAGINE: I AM THE ULTIMATE CONCLU-
sion of the allure of silk, the shimmer and the breeze of silks.
After all, my skin is silken, my grandmother's hands sheer as silk,
my mother's cherry-blond hair hard to picture without the capri-
cious play of light changing her thick mane of a coif moment to
moment from golden to cerise, ash blond to emboldened chest-
nut. These are but a few of the qualities of silk that are my blood,
my blood memory, my dreams. Yet without the extraordinary
vision of Ferdinand and Isabella, Cristóbal Colón would not
have been charged with the mission to find an alternate route to
India, thence China, where silk was born. Colón, Columbus, the
adventurer would not have set foot on Santo Domingo in search

of the *richesse* of silks and gold, then synonymous in the Old
World, never suspecting sugar, tobacco, rice and cotton would
be as gold to silk; that Africans, wrapped in a tight ivory co-
coon of bondage we call slavery, would inhabit these "Indies,"
an indigo damask demographic, fertile, furtive, hybrid, glisten-
ing as silk does when the moon changes phases, as we do under
a tropical sun. Silken and foreign to these shores and to the
thought, these are the origins of my genealogical essence, my
blood trail in the New World, another Silk Road.

Though my earliest recollection of all that is silk, all that swish
soft fondling fabric conveys, are perfumed and gliding over my
eyebrows in the depths of my mother Ellie's closet. What
shrouded my young head, braids and all, was the miracle of the
night, of conga drums, claves and castanets, formal dinners,
chandeliers of translucent swirls of lights dancing above the
heads of very important guests whose crepe, velvet, chiffon,
and silk I'd bask in under the dining table. So like an ocean of
unexpected sensation were the skirt hems tickling my shoulders, sometimes I'd forget to gaze at the ankles in silk stockings
that lent ordinary brown and bronze calves the magic of rose
quartz, moonstones, tourmaline sculpture, as secret as the next
brush stroke of Sonia Delaunay or Raoul Dufy turning silk
painting to a landscape abstractly worn by Parisian women adept at becoming art that could walk. While we in the New
World far from St.-Germain-de-Prés or Tours, ignorant of the
aroma and thick layers of medieval Venice, we drew La Habana
to us, as if the satin-bodiced and feathered brocatelle of the
mulatas at the Tropicana were more than our senses could bear,
enough to sate our sense of beauty and illicit treasures. Were
not the seeds of white mulberry trees upon which the silkworm

dined contraband, smuggled, hidden dangerous cargo transported by the foolish or foolhardy headstrong bent on wealth and stature? But we needn't concern ourselves with distant and ancient menace. The flickering of home-style black-and-white movies after the flan, after the cigars and cognac, bringing lampas-skinned brown beauties swinging from trees, swinging their hips was intimidating enough. Surely, there was no one more beautiful than a woman in silk smiling down at me from a gargantuan Cuban cypress tree, while I hid at the foot of the stairs waiting for the exception.

As I understood with the mind of a child befuddled by the Cold War and immersed in the films of WWII, my mother visited a fashion showroom not far from La Place de l'Opéra where an impish French model paraded in front of her as she sat, probably in chairs of chiné velvet with thickets of exotic plants, peacocks, and bizarre Oriental leitmotifs. As she sat admiring the models, my father, Paul T., who was smooth as silk, decided upon a white silk taffeta strapless sheath embossed with pearls, with a flying panel of the same materials, that I now know to be a "robe à la française" so that my mother's figure was virginal, salacious, and regal at one and the same time. A velvet cape with the same pearled pattern was strewn over her left shoulder as she mysteriously moved down the winding staircase. I was speechless, not because I'd been found out, but because I was sure I was not to see my mother in such a state of ethereal sensuality in my lifetime. I almost believed the glow on her face was a reflection of the moon flirting unabashed in front of my father. My father who was as smooth as silk, though not named "Silk" like so many others of us. His muscular frame interacted with the world as something precious to behold, beyond the possibility of an ordinary anything. This couple slipping into a black Missouri night to hear the raw silk voice of Tina Turner, the velvet ciselé intonations of Gloria Lynne or the heightened bouclé of Maria Callas were mine. I came from this phenomenon, as Toomer said "rare as a November cotton flower".

in search of a home

I HAVE MOVED SO MANY TIMES, FROM UPSTATE NEW York to Alabama and back to New Jersey before I was even seven, that home has to be something other than a place.

I was fortunate enough to have been born in an America that was a formidably, egregiously and fecund black one. My life and dreams were segregated at first by a law and then by choice. With a daughter in hand to raise, I had no idea how to fashion a healthy "integrated" lifestyle, so I went looking for the tried and true, a black one like the one I knew.

If I consult either Freud or Fanon, my sense of home is problematic. I'd really no place to be anybody but in the syncopated double-entendres of the music I heard in my house: Little

Richard, Little Willie John, Ellington, Hawkins, and the Paragons in their terribleness.

I am living now in an old chocolate factory just the other side of the Delaware River, the Ben Franklin Bridge off-ramp, and a wind's caprice of wafts of tomato, chicken noodle, or newfangled manhandler split pea with ham from Camden's Campbell's Soup or its Dominican merengues haunting Penn's Landing as Machito and Piaf, the Seine: it is an eccentric amalgam of all the places I've ever made my own. I've held on to a few of my singular icons: the papier-mâché siren with two missing teeth and a scarf Aunt Jemima would covet from Barranquilla; the bronze dreads of a twenty-first-century Neo-rasta; a cherry wood silhouette of my daughter at 2 months enlarged to mythological proportions; and my spinning wheel from New Hope.

All these things remind me that I've come from somewhere, a great many "wheres," which will inform and shape what I make of this new territory, Philadelphia.

My home is now across the alley from the Painted Bride, an alternative performance space, where many of my dance and New Black Music contemporaries appear not infrequently. My band, Syllable, even performed there last spring. Yet, the daily clip of a walk I make from my flat to the nearest bodega seemed to me, when I was a stranger, leaden, never-ending, an affront to my tastes for streets jammin' to Puente or James Brown. When I first passed the hollowed-out bottom of the Bridge, I felt like a trespasser, off-beat and out-of-tune. Trepidation and a sense of illegitimacy swirled about me, like an eddy in the river yet to befriend me. I didn't hear Langston whispering of the rivers he'd known; nor Lee Andrews and the Hearts asking for a second chance.

This is me, the same woman who walks wrapped in remembering phrases of poetry, of music, with no more aplomb than boarding the local train. The same woman who wouldn't consider not living near a live-music venue or an after-hours club.

So, the sear of the avant-garde as established by Coltrane, Tyner and Murray is across the alley and I haven't once ventured beyond its threshold. Yes, I am inspired by Geri Allen's intricately challenging piano, as well as, Pat Hall-Smith's careening spirited choreography. But then, I missed both Dennis Brutus and Margaret Randall. I've not abandoned my friends or the wonders they create. It's just this is where I live. I'll see them along Seventh Avenue South in New York, walking the streets of Brixton or in Managua or Taso at dust. They are my landmarks, better my passports, to the rest of the world. If I succumb and rush to see them so close to me, my fragile cosmological paradigm would condense to a black hole. Overwhelmed by the energy, the density of the implications of their lives and work, I'd collapse. Sun Ra of the Heliocentric Arkestra lives here already. He conjures up desires to walk on the Moon in a zoot suit with the colored people from Mars and Jupiter. No. Other people must stay where they were, so I can invent who I am, undistracted. They should keep ahold to the gifts they bear until I can somehow leave Philadelphia, pay my respects and pick up my presents.

Trying to establish how long ago or how I got to Philadelphia is difficult. Not because I'm forgetful or imprecise, but actually living anywhere in America is something I'd just as soon not contemplate. Yet, three or four times a week, I hustle past Independence Square with its cadre of bonneted and demure guides eager to take any and all of us through the sacred hall where the Founding Fathers wrangled in humidity that baffled all but a slave's metabolism to complete a document that defined me and mine as no more than 3/5 human. When that bothers me viscerally, I hurry up to Market Street to the Graff House, hidden in "New Philadelphia" steel and glass, where Jefferson wrote the Declaration of Independence. I can rest my heels for a minute. Then I realize I'm on the south side of Market. South Philly means Dion and the Belmonts, Paul Anka, Frankie Avalon, and Dick Clark's America where white people danced and we entertained with no bitterness. I hear Chubby Checker gleefully: "Come on baby, let's do the Twist" ... we can change the way they clap or how they boogie up to each other, but fried eggs in Woolworth's—never.

Running again to someplace beautiful, I maneuver myself to the Horticultural Society where a sweet gentlemanly black man of the old school lets me wander the colonial gardens before the public is allowed, as if protecting me from the befuddled glances of Japanese tourists who simply can't understand what I would be doing there. There in the pristine order of roses at right angles I see the Capris singing woefully, *Only God Knows.* Two guys and a girl and a piano wooing the world with the legato strains of a du-wop more related to *Nobody Knows* ... than Frankie Lymon.

But there's always Betsy Ross' house by the International Seamen's Union across from my bodega where the wayward, the whimsical, and the exiled can feed the pigeons, nibble a warm pretzel with mustard or watch clouds cavort. It's safe here for a while, until I'm mistaken for a homeless person even though I can sew.

I regally escort myself from the scene to the Quintones crooning *Down the Aisle of Love* or if I'm feeling sassy I saunter off to Maureen Gray's *Dancin' in the Strand.* That's why I can't pinpoint how long I've been here, where Ben Franklin is buried. Nicky Scarfo Jr. was shot down in front of my daughter's school, three black men were beat at a bus stop because some Italian's sister's gold chain was ripped off by some other black man earlier in the day, and the Friends' Meeting House is home to a man who knows God personally, but defecates, curses, riles and preaches the rising of a blood-drenched moon till sleep overtakes him.

You can find me in the history and the music of this place: the whoops and hollars of Mother Bethel A.M.E. Church, the whines and labyrinthine solos of Shepp and Ayler during my escapades at the Third Street Jazz and Rock Store. You can find me in the throes of Schoolly D and Jazzy Jeff. I luxuriate in our audacity. And maybe I've come upon a site that can support the weight of my past, the past of my people, in concrete terms. I've been grinning all upside myself, since I spent a couple of mornings hauling tree limbs loosed by Hurricane Hugo from Society Hill back to my house. These gnarled, asymmetrical and intermingled species handed up to me by winds direct from Charleston hang over my head at night, where I rest secure that the Carolinian spirits of my grandparents and their great-grandparents protect me ferociously in a gracious manner. From Lombard where my church is over to Pine Street in Society Hill, Du Bois came upon the community he documented in *The Philadelphia Negro,* Richard Allen argued for unequivocal emancipation, and the mannered dames of Bill Gunn's *Forbidden City* eschewed riffraff. And as Buckwheat or Farina might say, "Heah I comes" with my tree limbs, the pulse of Barbara George's song *I Know (You Don't Love Me No More)* and my hightops amidst so much of what I come from.

But my neighborhood is not an abstraction. My father caught the bus to Lincoln University at 10th and Arch and the hordes of Philadelphia's black sun-seekers rolled into Atlantic City where we sought each other's gleaming bodies at the world-famous "Chickenbone Beach" or late in the night nigh sun-up we'd fall into the bright neon of Kentucky Avenue's Club Harlem where the Philly Sound was swaggering, romantic, and cold-blooded. The Delfonics in aqua capes and silver sequins performed miracles for us: we were not only gang wars and pressed heads awkward in the summer sun. We had what we thought was "style" and we were "bad."

Aside from Quakers, Philadelphia is a mass of hurtin' folks. From Katharine Hepburn's Main Line gamine to itinerant residents of Fishtown calling the police to report black men prowling corner telephone booths. At the same time white guys from South Jersey and Philadelphia would have us believe that when they strut, the same dust flies and the sun get out their way. But only an Italian from these parts could call me from Oregon, the lands of Coltrane frame-by-frame, to say that George Clinton of Parliament-Funkadelic walked through the door, saw all the (black) people, made a swift about-face, and slapped five with the only white boy in the place cause they shared synchronous galactic rotations. Here I am, divorced Bride of Frankenstein, whose child in the womb was definitively "under a Groove," leaping between Cecil Taylor's fingers and possessed with the Holy Ghost à la Clara Ward, simultaneously watching this boy pull his pants highter above his waist than they already were, leaning backwards with his shoulders hunched forward for good form. Like he doesn't know Jerry Blavat, "the Geator with the Heater," would have been shot dead guarding Don Corleone if we hadn't offered him and his kind Vinnie Terranova, who got a little too much Brooklyn for me, but when he gets to Atlantic City he's somebody I know.

Seriously, Paris and Philadelphia are cities to walk, linger and seduce alone. There's no need to make friends or tolerate loneliness. At Deux Magots de Beauvoir and Sartre converse near me. Here I stroll Pine Street with Alice Dunbar-Huff. I am surrounded by my literary and hoodlum antecedents. There's no room for a casual affair or an intimate friend to draw me from this incredible actuality. I live in the breath of my familial and unconscious myths. I trace their footsteps, hear the lilt of their voices, manifest our anger, loose in the crushingly colored insularity of all their love. One friend told me that blacks in Philadelphia just don't like white people. Personally, I think they just don't like anybody who isn't, as they say, who we be.

So in the true tradition of a city slicker in my own right, I've found a way to pull one over on them and the rest of the country I ambivalently call home, by experiencing my nation-state in "house" music. This is three turntable, state-of-the-art quadrupled multiple bass lines, with Ayleresque solos weaving in and out of sophisticated scratching, and wails of post–Fontella Bass voices that force movements more staples in Rio or Dakar than Haddonfield. It is seriously colored. So colored in fact that the last all-night club I went to, the Outer Limits, appropriately enough, the three white people who had the nerve to approach the dance floor sat down in less than two minutes and didn't get up until dawn, when they left. In this blood-churning sweat-evoking rhythm is a cultural thickness that can't be penetrated, translated or turned out thirty years later in a cleaned-up version like, say, New Kids on the Block. This is no less an art or subterfuge than the Underground Railroad: you just left, listened to the strains of spirituals, caught the movement of those around you, and were gone even if you don't know where to. This is a kind of improvisation. In the land of "house" music we have an indelible home, an anthem, an eclectic unrepeatable march to ourselves. Incontrovertibly in my own backyard, I don't have to excuse myself, wonder if any other black people are coming, or pace my choice of words. In fact the "niggahfied" aura the "house music" clubs in my neighborhood lend to the colonial vestiges

about me thrill my soul. I can tell the boys in Jersey romping
the suburbs doing the Bristol Stomp to come on down my way
where they can meet the Orlons on South Street or the young
black boys who dazzle gravity with their feet. We let anybody
know, who's got the gall to cross our paths: "Oh we gonna house
you."

however you come to me

I HAVE NOT ENTERED A RELATIONSHIP WITH ANY MAN in the last twenty years in which I did not fully expect to blow to smithereens the myth of phallocentrism that buoys the dismal personal prospects of women snared by the guy on the white horse. I confess that few of my consorts were toppled from the patriarchal thrones of their imaginations, but I am certain that the volatility of most of my relationships with English-speaking African American men can be attributed to intense ontological struggles: whose universe is this?

Ever the optimist, I set up households with a number of fellas, only to discover that: 1) If we are both artists, his work comes first and laundry and dinner are my responsibility; 2) If I am doing fairly well in my profession, this is construed as an affront of some kind that must be acted out with continued references to my good luck; 3) Differences of opinion on esthetic, political, or philosophical matters are invalid because I just don't know what I am talking about. These are all common, sometimes comical, defenses of relationships that institutions like marriage or cohabitation enforce to sustain the male entity like the Federal Reserve assists the economy. Having been referred to as money in the bank more than once, I can assure you it is not a compliment.

Alas, on this planet the nexus of women as money, women as property, women as entertainment, has not yet been dissolved. So, no matter how much we work against it or attempt to free our particular relationships from it, we are functioning in societies that require our diminution at any cost to us. For decades we have known that we are in the most grave danger of being maimed or killed by men who are our lovers or husbands, not some stranger. Yet we spend years of culturally conditioned inactivity dreaming about these affairs that double our chances to die violently. They've done a great job here, on us and on our daughters. Still, I have not opted for lesbian separatism or celibacy as a lifelong avocation. Why not?

I like men.

They're sexy, funny, exciting. They've got hair in weird places. They can give me great pleasure: intellectually and sexually. On a fast bop or a mambo, they can spin me round so I feel I have the grace and speed of an intergalactic nymph. They can show me how to catch a ball, or the problem with my left uppercut. I get a chance to pull out my evening bikinis with silver and red ostrich feathers or open crotches. My satin sheets take on the powers of monster roller coasters, of southwestern hot springs. Their eyes light up at candlelit suppers at the beach, gourmet omelets in the middle of the night. I can go on and on. The texture of their skin is different; they smell different. But the most important thing is that all this is given freely because it gives me pleasure.

I love my father and brother: canny, wise, and benevolent patriarchs, both. Yet the men I've chosen (some have chosen me) to be integrals of my fairly stable foothold in the family of the future are wondrous eccentrics who are just as uncomfortable with the stiff-upper-lip hierarchy of masculinity as I am.

In fact, men have always been of great significance in the twists and turns of my career from the beginning. I am saying this because it's important for us as women to know that there are men in this very world who do want us to flourish and who will help. What is real are friendships with extraordinary men that transcend the craft and business.

But men, poor things, would rather do without any of the above when that's possible rather than just enjoy it, because they think we function like they do. Dinner and dancing for them is a down payment on a piece of ass. A piece of pussy comes with a drive to the shore. A gift is a ransom for your body, my dear, not a token of affection. That's why they say things like: "You shouldn't have done all this for me"; "I don't celebrate birthdays"; "All this fancy stuff don't do nothin' for me." Of course not, it can't. If they enjoy any of the fruits of our culinary or sensual imagination upfront, that means they owe us: their bodies, which are the home of their penises, which are the raison d'être for their superiority, which gives their souls the power to reign over all creatures small and large. So the keen disappointment we feel when one of our fancies shoves the water chestnuts around on his plate like it was warmed-over spinach, or cursorily glances at a negligee that was two weeks' salary, is not a manifestation of the foolhardiness of romance, but rather evidence that our attempts to be special, if only to ourselves, must be stymied. Ordinary is the call of the day. There was nothing to it. Nothing is going on of significance. It was an ordinary day. Nothing happened.

I don't like to have days of my own that are singularly nondescript. I take this to mean I am on spiritual retreat, which is sometimes necessary, or I am at the beginning of a depression if I don't do something about my state of mind. In other words, what we may take to be genuine healthy interest in making our experiences unique or pleasurable, men experience as investments of ransom for their attentions like we weren't there, too.

I mean, there are men who are honest enough to buy those life-size plastic dollies with an opening where a vagina should be that's filled with a sponge they can dampen. So we, in fact, are not there, and their experience is wholly their own. But most men like to actually have us there, believing that our reality is subsumed.

Years ago our lack of prescience actually encouraged the hop-in-and-out school of lovemaking, which also assumed that we as women had taken birth control pills or used diaphragms, IUDs, or "whatever." The "whatever" always took me aback. I tried to imagine that I was an exotic beast that needed a "whatever" or some Byzantine contraption that required a "whatever," but those ideas were off the mark. "Whatever" was anything or nothing that I had procured to protect my partner from what would inevitably have been "my" pregnancy. Remember the sacred phrases: "Well, I thought you were using something"; "Weren't you using anything?" "Well, whatever."

Ordinary. Disembodied. Nameless. Pussy. Safety in nonspecificity.

My brother.

These days the language isn't quite so abstract. Most men know they should use nonoxynol-treated latex condoms to save their own lives or ours, but they have very little understanding of STDs or the HIV virus. Some believe that fucking fast mitigates the virus. Others hold the belief that only sperm ejaculated into the vagina, not sperm that oozes into our mouths, is dangerous. Once again, since pussy is some independent organs *sans* female, they don't connect that women have two mouths: both are vulnerable to the implications of unprotected sex. Oh, I must not leave out the gooey eyes, the masculine set jaw and pout that accompany a guy who is accepting his fate to put a condom on; all grim and purposeful. Can it really be my fault that his sensual vocabulary is so limited that if there's no raw penetration this boy can't have any fun? Obviously not. But there's even one more nonsensical than that. There are men out there who believe that lists of previous lovers extracted by interrogations, pilfering of diaries, gossip, visitations from li'l birds, can assure them of which one of us (with the pussy) is HIV-positive and which ones aren't. None of these fellas has a certifiable belief in magic, either.

As we delve further into male erotic esoterica, we must deal with the idea of male shape-shifters, though as far as I can tell it is a purely metaphorical experience. They think their penis is their fist or a celery stalk. They think our pussy is their pussy, but they're not quite sure because they continually inquire: "Whose pussy is this?" Sometimes they do this with great alarm and ferocity in their voices. If some of us are wont to touch ourselves to enhance our own pleasure, these very same fellas may demand to know what we are doing with their nipple, their clit, their bush, which apparently were appropriated without knowledge or consent. I, myself, never had any interest in transmogrification until I saw how exponentially content men became when they believed they had their own pussies.

One last note, however. Having the pussy has in no way refined their knowledge of what to do with one: their own or anybody else's. Although I must give credit to the one or two I know who are so adept I never doubt for a second that they are all over and through me and I know he's putting that Trojan on, but I don't know when or how. Oh, it's exhilarating to be with a man who wants me, wants this together sweating and tide-rising to be seamless, uninterrupted, sweet, satisfying, and specifically what we are doing with each other: the breath and time we take to look, to gaze and giggle: good safe sex.

mr. wrong

"nothin' from nothin' leaves nothin'"
"we're off to see the wizard, the wonderful wizard of oz ..."
"you gotta have somethin' if you wanna have somethin' with me"
*"a wonderful wizard he is because, because of the wonderful things
    he does"*

FOR MANY YEARS I HAVE LIVED IN A STATE OF SUS-
pended disbelief as well as elaborate models of the cinderella
complex & just plain old guilt that i had done much better
than my peers, especially my male colleagues. a self-identified
feminist, my work reflected, & to this day reflects, a sense of
urgency in complex examinations of the nature of heterosexual
relations in the first decade of the 21st century. but i must con-

fess i have not always or virtually ever lived up to my own ideals. that is why i led into this essay with a tangle of bill withers & judy garland. what a mess i have made. & then there is my faulty memory of what i was complicit in as well & relationships i had no intention of honorably tending to. now i find myself chuckling about situations so many years have passed & i have moved on & started over again with no male helping who wasn't also being paid by the housekeeper. i find myself raising my eyebrows & doing strange things with my eyeballs now that i want to reveal my malice & begrudging in situations i knew to be unsettling & humiliating to my so-called partner of the moment.

it was inevitable. my career had peaked way before that of my alleged peers & i created an entire slew of gigolos, sycophants, & angry black an puerto rican loves whose aim was to get whatever they could wrangle from me before i understood betrayal. yet i survived again. the concerted attacks on my commitment to afro-americans & black latins took a terrible toll on me. i grew to be suspicious of the intentions of many who crossed my integrity boundaries, yet i was not always able to stand my ground. things just moved too fast for a young man to catch.

for instance there was a black puerto rican independista who came to me seeking a safe house where his wounds could be tended to & arrangements for his transport out of the city could be made swiftly. luckily i could do all that, but months later after he returned to the city, i lent him $200. many months later, the check he wrote back to me was for "mizfullashit." there are many instances of that kind of exploitation. a man who i began to love went into a rage because i had several hundred dollars on hand when i went to buy fresh crabs at a harlem fishery. this fella wanted to know how come some woman could have all that money to buy fresh crabs for a party i was giving to which he

had not been invited because he was a definitely married man &
i had no need to bother his wife or children with the fact that i
was briefly this man's mistress. nevertheless, this same guy kept
up his chorus of "whose pussy is this," which i found laughable,
but i replied ever compliant "oh so & so this is yours" & he
would settle down. he really lost my respect & understanding
when he flew into a fury as i prepared myself to be the mistress
of ceremonies at a celebration of cuba's moncada barracks day, of
singular importance to the cuban people as the day fidel landed
first on the shores of western cuba. this man actually believed
his tirade as a black anglo-saxon was going to stop me. the last
thing i remember hearing from the top of the stairs was "what
about me, what about me." And this is not the last time i'd hear
this query.

i find that monolingual african american men are truly undone
by multilingual black women, not just me. i find my commitment to african americans in this hemisphere compelling as
opposed to a direct ontological belief in the mother land which
disturbs our men beyond comprehension. but one of my so-
called partners transgressed my boundaries to the degree that
he had to go, get out of my life, when he grabbed my tithing
card outta my hands & threw it into the trash. even then i understood this to be an egregious breach of my human rights & i
took my daughter with the clothes on our backs & small suit-
cases, allegedly to visit my family, though we would not be
coming back. there are so many instances of my acquiescence
to bizarre behaviors that i am wont to reveal. some i'm sure will
show up in my creative endeavors but i want to help unmask
the terror of the patriotic as it manifests itself in our lives. i almost forgot a fella who gave me a day at the spa with nails,
manicure, steam baths, hairdo, the works & i thought that was

wonderful until i found a wonderfully decorated box at my hotel room that held a black leather bustier & a ping-pong paddle. then there was another one who kept a machete in a loft above my head & he was very forceful during sex to the extent that my gynecologist told me i had to stop seeing him because of the black & blue marks on my arms which indicated to her domestic violence which frightened me. this scared me so he had to go. i haven't lived with a man or chased after one for many years & i have been reasonably just fine. i survived & any woman who is living with some one of these men: tread softly, get out & shut the door. when a fella attempts to take control of our bodies, our politics or our god, believe me he might just kill us.

justice

INITIALLY, I WAS DEMONICALLY TICKED AT THE NOTION that I, Ntozake Shange, a.k.a. Paulette Linda Williams, whose American birth certificate from an alleged Union state, New Jersey, read "colored" in 1948, was asked to write a piece about justice. This was truly laughable, since it is quite clear to me that "justice" as a fact, fantasy, or concept is so removed an actuality in my life, intellectual as well as visceral, that I thought maybe I should try my hand at a myth or my first science fiction. But the blues has not always made me or my people unhappy, you see; this idea is false. The general ideas roaming American minds—black, white, Asian, Chicano, Texan, urban, empty of truth whichever they are about who and what I come from and what is "just" for us—are as scary as the bullet holes of Huey Long's assassination in Baton Rouge and as sad as the Trail of Tears, and I haven't gotten to "the Negro" yet. We are essentially a generous people, not eager to chasten or exploit. But I can say right here and now that the absence of a day in honor of the end of slavery in this country is shameful, which to my mind makes it unjust—the opposite of justice.

To my mind, justice is inconceivable where there is ignorance, yet the truth of the inescapable essential ties of the slave trade to the so-called Renaissance, the evolution of an industrial workforce, and the globalization of trade, economics, and politics is a thought "foreign" to the American mind. The word "manumission" cannot be used in ordinary conversations; references to the Freedmen's Project are left hanging in the awkward silence of lack of knowledge the way our bodies hung from tree limbs for days and nobody saw nothin' to cut down. Far and away the most painful aspect of this wishful absenting of Africans from "our" own history is the terrible isolation experienced by those of us who are descendants of Diaspora in the New World.

Only because my father wasn't W. E. B. Du Bois, Paul Robeson, or Walter White, I assume, he carried a valid American passport, as did my mother with whom he traveled. I am so lucky, fortunate, blessed to have seen actual footage (in black and white, no less) of Haitians, Dominicans, Costa Ricans, Congolese going about their daily business in modern times, using automobiles, electric radios, elevators, freeways, books; let's not forget books. I say this without aplomb because I was laughed at in all but a few of the schools I attended if I so much as suggested that: 1) there were Africans outside the United States who had not ever been owned by anyone, or 2) if they were property in some contorted system of justice, they did not necessarily speak

English, and 3) they voted and ate in restaurants, went to librar-
ies and took buses, unlike any of the Negroes (I have no idea
what they called us out of my earshot) they knew—therefore,
I was really a silly little ninny to speak of such absurdities as the
lives of black folk. Even then, our longing for our song, our
place on the face of the earth, summarily dismissed.

Slavery was such a long time ago.

Why can't I forget about all that and get on with my life?
I'd like to, believe me. But, not unlike other humans who suffer
trauma or brain-washing (a very popular phrase during my
childhood), I was raised surrounded by public images of people
who looked like me, who looked and acted like what I was told
slaves, at least the black ones, looked and acted like. Right after
the first television sets were available commercially, I was apparently watching cartoons with my mother, who shut the
thing off. "Why, Mom? Why?" I cried. The answer made no sense
to me then. She said something I don't remember, but I instinctively recall the uncontestable. Mother, Eloise Williams, wrote
the network that the cartoon with Epamimondas chasing himself around a tree till he caught up with his own stereotypical
Ubangi lips, which turned into pancakes that he smacked as
black and unhappy as poor Uncle Tom never knew, was inap-
propriate for modern America. Yet, Buckwheat and the Little
Rascals regularly performed impromptu minstrel shows blackface and all. *The Jazz Singer* featuring Eddie Cantor, of course,
introduced me to the history of Yiddish theater, the plight of
southern Europeans on the Lower East Side, and the absolute
distain held for what I came from by everyone in the world, I
imagined. Everybody knew, even I, that Paul Henreid, Tyrone
Power, Errol Flynn, and James Cagney had saved the world
over and over in moving black-and-white frames from fascism
and hatred of differences. It was very clear to me that whoever I

was and wherever I came from had an extremely tenuous relationship to other living things, besides cotton, cane, sleeping cars, shoeshine stands, bozo's unshined shoes, gorillas on the Empire State Building, heads of unknown colored people decorating Carolinian roads for pleasure, for a laugh, for terror? I don't know.

I'm beginning to feel like the homeless man who haunts and taunts residents of the Upper West Side. I am lost in the confoundment of what it is I'm supposed to be, do, say, respect, cherish. I want to make some noise and bash some heads. Run the Boers into the sea. Take all the Ashante art out the basement of the British Museum, out the basement of the Met for that matter. When I talk about what I imagine to be just, I sound like a crazy niggah roaming the streets and dangerous to American "civilization" (I have heard it called that, "civilization"). Anyway, I'm a doctor's daughter who was presented to "society" at the Waldorf, who graduated from a Seven Sister College, and I'm just as lacking in understanding American justice as Bessie Smith on her way to a hospital that took colored, or Emmett Till's mother. I'm not even close to approaching the gall and ungracious sadism demonstrated when white folks ask, "Well, what's it like to be, uh, 'black in America'?"

But it was all so long ago. The whole country is going wild cause a niggah allegedly kicked a white woman. Entire news editorials stunned by the burning of black churches, the mutating of young black men's souls and bodies on the sidewalks with the police and the tech crew from *Cops*, or in the crack houses and heroin dens with the skanks and steel doors protecting that high that lasts a few seconds. Affirmative action is a ploy by the white man how? Well, how low can you go? Oh, that's right, Al

Campanis already declared scientifically that however low white men go, niggahs don't float, so we must be at the bottom.

I'm actually "justified" in thinking that's how white folks think. My father was told he should study another language besides French because his lips were so thick. This decades after Léon Dumas and Léopold Senghor gave French language an entire new idiom, "Negritude." My mother once had a fiancé who promised he could take her away "from all this." "What?" she asked her white devotee. "Why, from having to be colored." These are only two examples of how justice has been offered to my family. There's one more I mustn't leave out. A second-generation Polish teacher persuaded my parents that my sister, who ran like the wind or Wilma Rudolph, really should not pursue track and field because so many Negros do that. Oh.

I wish Dinesh D'Souza had been in my front yard that night when somebody white came with a firebomb. I wish Dinesh D'Souza had picked up one of his relative's bodies from the banks of the Little Geechee River or the side of an Alabama road with his genitals cut out, or just go to worship in a church, now ashes. Or, simply live off Hwy. 59 in Houston where some Anglo woman shouts, "Can't you niggags just f—— get out my way." We were crossing the street, my child and I, on the green light with the walking white neon person in plain view. My baby was not yet two, but she'd had her ultimate American experience, when this white woman who was making a left turn shouted, "Niggahs, just get the hell out my way." And my baby was still in her stroller. So we move downtown and they tear that down. We got to get work, but the work's moved outta town. They stopped the bus service because there were no more commuters. The suburbs were self-sufficient, except for day workers and menial laborers, and I figure we could get there anyway we could. After all, slaves got by on nothin', why can't you?

I don't wanna. So my escape from what is clearly a continuous assault on all my sensibilities is to talk myself out of it. Talk around the racism in English, Spanish, and French, enough to create a world to sustain me. I've found whatever I can call justice by forever returning to the root of a language, the design of a plantation, the workings of a sugar mill, the chants of street corner B-boys, the words of those before me—Garvey, Martí, Diop, Machel, and the images of Bearden, Barthé, Michaux. I have to scrape the bottoms of souls, dreams, nightmares, and syllables to taste what justice might possibly be.

porque tu no m'entrende?
whatcha mean you
can't understand me?

BEFORE WE CAN HONESTLY ADDRESS MULTI-CULTUR-
alism, we must address the issues of language, the ontological
chauvinism of the English language, which since medieval times
has found it necessary to refer to other languages such as Italian
or French as dandified and lacking depth or erudite beyone comprehension like Latin, while at the same time a greedy, swallow-
ing language which appropriates words and gestures as an infant
sucks milk at the nipple. Without examining our relationship to
the English language, we cannot honestly "hear" the "other"
speak, we cannot become intimate with what we do not respect.
What we deem as "foreign" we cannot take to our hearts.

As the Brazilian novelist Lydia Fagundes Telles notes in
Girl in the Photograph:

I used to think about my people. I knew I wouldn't go back
but I kept on thinking about them so much. Like when you
take a dress out of a trunk, a dress you're not going to be able
to wear, just to look at. To see what it was like. Afterwards
one folds it up again and puts it away but one never considers
throwing it away or giving it to anyone. I think that's what
missing things is.

The Middle Passage was not monolingual, nor were the grape
and lettuce fields, the avocado and cane fields of Florida and
Cuba and the Yucatán, nor the rice paddies of the Carolinas and
the Philippines and Vietnam, nor the rhythm and blues songs
of South Central LA, or Houston Vietnam-town. We have not
seen alone. We could not "hear." We are strangers to the black
Uruguayan voter polled on Galavision, to the Asian Cuban in
Machito's band, the Navajo weaver imagining mud cloth as an
alternative to what she's known so long.

Yet as monolingual African Americans, we've turned inward
on ourselves in order to be able to hear ourselves outside the
thunder of Sambo's visage and the blare of the Mammy's smile in
our faces. We try to create and re-create ourselves as did 16th-
century Peruvians, as Irene Silverblatt suggests in "Becoming
Indian":

> Early hints of Indian: identities appear in the Andes three
> decades after the Spanish invasion, when, in 1565, the Taki
> Onqoy (Dancing Sickness), a movement of nativist redemp-
> tion, inspired women and men, kurakas and peasants in Pe-
> ru's central highlands. Signaling both the despair attending
> European doninion and the hope of being able to abolish
> it, Andean gods began to take over Andeans's souls. Those
> possessed by the dancing sickness blamed the deteriorating

condition of their lives (impossible labor demands and high morality) on themselves and other natives for deserting *huacas* (deity, sacred place) for Christian gods. To right the wrongs of this world, the Taki Onqoys argued, would require Andean peoples to return to their sacred traditions, to restore the sacred balance between huacas and mortals, and to renounce Christianity and all things Spanish. Huacas might have been defeated by Christian gods once, but now the tables would be turned. And their promised victory would be a total one: Spanish gods, completely routed, would disappear from the Andes and from native life.

If we would "rout" the White man from our lives, having delivered ourselves no way of naming the universe outside of the English language, where are we to go? In that sense, Clinton Turner Davis and Marta Vega are correct in suggesting that the Caribbean's a vital ever-erupting source of our myths, our spirit guides, our tragedies and triumphs. Even our rhythms survived Pizarro, Trujillo, Batista, and Pinochet as well. For we must never forget that there were no New World territories that escaped the presence of African bondage, of the slave trade of Africans who look just like us. The danger in seeing only ourselves in chains and only "knowing" English is one that Édouard Glissant discusses in *Selected Essays*: the universal language of music eases us into a language of our own.

When the large plantations of the southern United States collapse, the blacks begin the move that will lead them first to New Orleans (bars, brothels, riverboats), then to the great sprawling cities: Chicago or New York, where they will become the proletariat and our *_____ the lumpen proletariat and have to face the unrelenting industrial world of America.

At each of the stages of this process that I outline here, black music is reborn. Gospel and blues, New Orleans and Chicago style, Count Basie's big band, bebop, free jazz. This music progressively records the history of the community, its confrontation with reality, the gaps into which it inserts itself, the walls which it too often comes up against. The universalization of jazz arises from the fact that at no point is it an abstract music, but the expression of a specific situation . . . The Creole song in Martinique and the beguine in Guadeloupe are primarily manifestations of the world of plantations. When the system collapses, nothing replaces it. Neither massive urbanization, nor industrialization. The Martinican people remain in a state of suspension in time, before the present system of exchange makes them into a dependent community. Musical creativity, cut off from the imperative of reality, becomes folkloric (in the worst sense). It does not evolve toward newly adapted forms. The universalization of the beguine was real (it is even possible that it exercised a profound and more durable influence on Europe, for instance, than do salsa and reggae today), but this music is soon worn out.

The catastrophe of ignoring the unfamiliar, the exiled, the forgotten is more than a bit of wrestling with "something missing," it is the terror of becoming the embodiment of our own folklore set in time and not defined in our own terms. Perhaps the constant moving about of our people from Africa to the Caribbean to North, South, and Central America, then Detroit, El Paso, and Nueva York or Little Haiti is one of the many elements at work to save us from an inert reality, a real objectification of the "I" and "yo!"—ya no me voy: As Edward Said suggests to Salman Rushdie who's not everyone's darling:

"What happens to landless people? However you exist in the world, what do you preserve of yourselves? What do you abandon?" I find one passage particularly valuable, as it connects with many things I have been thinking about. "Our truest reality," he writes, "is expressed in the way we cross over from one place to another. We are migrants and perhaps hybrids, in but not of any situation in which we find ourselves. This is the deepest continuity of our lives as a nation in exile and constantly on the move."

He is writing, of course, about the Palestinian people, but could we have been sure? Could that not be us as well? Our métier is improvisation which is undeniable, not a natural physical ability we were intentionally taught but a highly complicated intellectual, spiritual and aesthetic response to the loss of control of our lives and our language/s. A so-called people without histories, art, even love for our children for that matter. We must break through these grids of colonial contrivance and discover who has truly been round and about us, who is round and about us.

My editor's uncle printed numbers for the Mafia in the 1950s in Rhode Island. He took the Fifth Amendment 87 times in front of the Kefauver Commission. Working-class and gay cultures are made comedic relief when there is certainly not always a ball of laughter associated with being gay or working class in North America.

What say ye to all this heathen nonsense?

Hoping that we might, in fact, find the time to learn one another's tongues and secrets, I taunt and tease and challenge you with Salman Rushdie:

So, in place of Jonah's womb, I am recommending the ancient tradition of making as big a fuss, as noisy a complaint about

the world as is humanly possible. Where Orwell wished quiet-
ism, let there be rowdyism: in place of the whale, the protest-
ing wail. If we can cease envisaging ourselves as metaphorical
foetuses, and substitute the image of a new-born child, then
that will be at least a small intellectual advance. In time, perhaps, we may even learn to toddle.

As beginning dancers we have no ego problems learning merely
to walk again. Hopefully we will humble ourselves to learn to
simply talk again.

Muchas gracias an buenas tardes.

letter to a young poet

       querida antigua eisa,
you almost got it/ you really did
'born of the blood of struggle' we all here/ even if we don't
know it/ what if poetry isn't enuf?
watchu gonna do then?
paint?
dance?
put your backfield in motion & wait for james brown to fall
    on his knees
like it's too much for him/ what?
too much for james?
yeah/ didn't you ever see the sweat from his brow/ a libation
    of passion

make a semi-circle fronta his body/ a half-moon of exertion
washin' away any hope he had of/ 'standin' it/ can't stand it
& he falls to his knees and three jamesian niggahs in a
     stroll
so sharp it hurts to bring him a cape that shines like the
     northern
star/ shinin' i say like you imagined the grease in the part of
     yr hair/
or yr legs/ or yr mother's face after rehearsal/ after she had you/
james falls to his knees cuz he 'cain't take it'/ he's pleadin'
'please/ please/ please/ don't go'
we look to see who brought james brown to the floor/
so weak/ we think/ so overwrought/ with the power of love
that's why poetry is enuf/ eisa/ it brings us to our knees
& when we look up from our puddles of sweat/
the world's still right there & the children still have bruises
tiny white satin caskets & their mothers weep like mary
     shda
there is nothing more sacred than a glimpse of the universe
it brought james brown to his knees lil anthony too/ even
     jackie wilson
arrogant pretty muthufuckah he was/ dropped/ no knee
     pads in the face
of the might we have to contend with/ & sometimes young
     boys bleed
to death face down on asphalt cuz fallin' to they knees was
     not cool/
was not the way to go/ it ain't/ fallin' to our knees is a public
     admission
a great big ol' scarlet letter that we cain't/ don't wanna escape any
feelin'/ any sensation of bein' alive can come right down on
     us/ & yes my tears & sweat

may decorate the ground like a veve in haiti or a sand
    drawing in melbourne/ but in the
swooning/ in the delirium/ of a felt life

can ya stand up, chile?

the point is not to fall down & get up dustin' our bottoms/
i always hated when folks said that to me/ the point
virginia—eisa/ is you fall on your knees & let the joy of
    survivin'
bring you to yr feet/ yr bottom's not dirty/ didn't even graze
    the earth/
no it's the stuff of livin' fully that makes the spirit of the poem

let you show yr face again & again & again

i usedta hide myself in jewelry or huge dark glasses
big hats long billowin' skirts/ 'anything' to protect me/ from
    the gazes
somebody see I'd lived a lil bit/ felt somethin' too terrible
    for casual conversation
& all this was obvious from lookin' in my eyes/ that's why i
    usedta read poem after poem
with my eyes shut/ quite a treat/ cept the memories take
    over & leave
my tequila bodyguard in a corner somewhere out the way of
    the pain
in my eyes that simply came though my body/ they say
my hands sculpt the air with words/ my face becomes the
    visage of a
character's voice/ i don't know
i left my craft to chance & fear someone wd see i care too much

take me for a chump
laugh & go home

this is not what happened

is poetry enuf to man a picket line/ to answer phones at the
rape crisis center/ to shield women entering abortion clinics
    from demons with
crosses & illiterate signs defiling the horizon at dawn/ to
    keep our children
from believing that they can buy hope with a pair of
    sneakers or another nasty
filter for a cheap glass pipe/ no/ no/ a million times no

but
poetry can bring those bleeding women & children outta
    time
up close enuf for us to see/ feel ourselves there/ then the
    separations
what makes me/ me & you// drops away & the truth that we
    constantly
avoid/ shut our eyes/ hold our breath hopin' we won't be
    found out/
surfaces darlin'/ & we are all everyone of those dark &
    hurtin' places/
those dry bloodied memories are no less ours than the
    mournin'/ yes
the mournin' we may be honorable enuf to endure with our
    eyes open/
the coroner cannot simply bring her hand gently down our
    eyelids/ leavin'
us to silence of not life/ the solitude of the unreachable

can ya stand up, 'chile'?
hands stretched out to touch again
not so you can get up & conquer the world/
you did that when you cdnt raise you head & yr body
    trembled so/
you scared yr mama/ that was when the poem took over &
    gave you back
what you discovered you didn't haveta give up/
all that fullness of breath/ houdini in an emotional maze/
    free at last
but nobody can see how you did it/ how'd she get out/
nobody'll know less you tell em/
do you really wanna write/
from twenty thousand leagues under a stranger's wailin?
can you move gracefully randomly thru the landmines that
are yr own angola/ hey you bosnia/ falujah!
are you shamed sometimes there's no feelin' you
can recognize in yr left leg? does the bleeding you'll do
    anyway
offend you or can you make a sacred drawing like ana
    medieta that will
heal us all? do i believe in magic?

hell yeah.
shd you?
i don't know.
don't know how yr gonna find yr way out the maze/ ancient
    as it is
no one can tell you the secret/ not me/ not aunt angela/ not
    yr mama
beautiful as she is. i usedta watch her legs cut through space
    like a ninja in ballet

shoes/ i wanted to be tall & clear-eyed like yr mama/ & you
    come tellin' me
i cd beat you up in a school-yard/ no
my daddy wda bought the school-yard & paid kids not to
    hurt me/
so what you see is not what you get
i am not a poem/ i am savannah's mother/ savannah sat
    with her bottle thru
the children's class at stanze's once we moved to texas/ but i
    was always
lookin' for your mother's legs to come slicing the air/ ten
    years later/ 2000 miles
away/ ed mock dead. tower of power fallen/ sly stone
    disappeared/ oakland like the back
of my hand/ now unknown/ 'get it & feel good' i usedta say
sometimes still do. difference is i cherish stupid lil things
    now/ did yr mama
tell you raymond asked our whole class after a bout with
    possessed drummers and
gravity/ if we ever took our dance clothes off/ he could smell
    us comin' cross the
bay bridge/ he shouted & pranced like some kinda stallion/
    like his sweat didn't
stink too/ workin' in the other realm is dirty work/ makes
    us smell bad/ did yr
mama tell ya? i know she didn't let ya believe makin' art was
    not a messy business/
she can't have/ we were trained too well

is poetry enuf, eisa?
that's gonna be up to you.
is poetry enuf for me?

why do you think i wrote 'for colored girls'?
i wanted y'all to come out from under yr starched pinafores &
    pressed heads
with some notion of dream & sanctity of spirit/
looks like some of it worked
but remember I'm still writin' still dancin'
fell on my knees so many times now/ i wrote rev. ike for a
    prayer cloth
it's serious like that
peaceful like that
i sweat when i write/ do you?

> the original aboriginal dancin' girl
> love,
> tozake

first love

i always knew i liked poetry more than anything, more than boys, more than butterflies, more than fresh sheets on a hot st. louis night. i'm not sure i liked poetry more than dancin' or jackie wilson, or even sleeping on the 2nd floor screened porch when even fresh sweet dried sheets were no match for the weight of the air on my sister's wandering limbs.

my mother, eloise, had benefited from what were then callt "elocution" lessons, privately given in the home of a striking, yet demure southern woman once removed to the bronx. There she mastered whitman, whittier, wheatley, shakespeare, and dunbar. this eclectic mix of word crafters were my lullabies, soothing rhymes, and demonstrations of slowly garnered memorization skills. this, i suspect is where my love of poets began. they served a purpose, even, in the short but widely lived life of a small colored child in east trenton where the houses and trees were as small as my arms' reach to my mind or later in the magnificence of a st. louis dawn i heralded the coming light with words, just as my mother had greeted me. these are the very beginnings of my romance with language. at least i can go back with a reasoned mind no further.

but mine was no constant love. i flirted with baudelaire and artaud because i longed for some immersion in dream. my life in the midst of the civil rights movement's beginnings when children played a fundamental role was highly irrational. racism is irrational and therefore my environs were fraught with absolute craziness. surrealism by thirteen was actually a grounding influence, which makes me smile now. even today if I'm besieged by pressures beyond my control off i go in search of a "dada."

to get more to the point of why i am the kind of poet i am, i have to remind you that i have always been a performing poet. i believed from my euro-american training that the greeks were right. poetry must be heard. i knew as a black person that when i asked somebody for a poem i didn't mean for them to give me a book, i meant for them to "deliver" it, say it, make it jump, fire the air with power and magic. this was always. i didn't say to myself, "i want to do that . . . i want to be a poet." until i saw amiri baraka and the spirit house movers. i'd grown to love leroi jones because of the delicacy of preface to a 20-volume suicide note, but the music and cultural textures that the spirit house movers offered on *1960 something . . .* or the lines "ruby dee weeps at the window/ being what we all will be/ sentimental bitter . . ." like love songs to a people, like a personal serenade from an absolute stranger who took my heart. that's when i knew i could say, "i want to do that."